PRAISE FOR *THE SAMSON SYNDROME*

I could not put this book down. Every page was riveting. Why?
Because I saw myself on every page. And you will too. This book will
change your life. Start reading immediately.

—PAT WILLIAMS
Senior Vice President of the Orlando Magic
and Author of *How to Be Like Mike* and *Unsinkable*

The Samson Syndrome is clear, biblical, practical, and packed with
perspective. Mark Atteberry helps us see the Samson in ourselves . . .
and take conscious steps to become the men Christ wants us to be.

—RANDY ALCORN
Author of *Safely Home* and *The Treasure Principle*

There is some 'Samson' in each of us. Mark Atteberry very clearly
helps us realize the downside of our strengths. My prayer for each
reader is that we will be . . . big enough to admit our mistakes . . . smart
enough to profit from them . . . and strong enough to correct them.

—JOHN C. MAXWELL
Founder of The INJOY™ Group and
New York Times Best-selling Author of
The 21 Irrefutable Laws of Leadership

Mark Atteberry has written the ultimate textbook for men. He covers
every issue every one of us faces every day. Warning: if you read this
book you will never be the same.

—JERRY COLANGELO
Chairman and CEO of the
Arizona Diamondbacks and the Phoenix Suns

How many books have you read that help you identify your weaknesses and then leave you hanging and feeling depressed wondering what to do about them? Not this one! Mark Atteberry, in his book *The Samson Syndrome,* helps target those issues and gives great practical suggestions to work through each. I'm truly impressed with this book! Although written for men, women can also benefit greatly from Mark's insights and applications. A must read!

—BOB RUSSELL

Senior Minister of Southeast Christian Church,
Louisville, Kentucky

Based on the story of Samson, Mark Atteberry lays out a map of hazards to avoid as you walk through life. If you want to fulfill all of your God-given potential, read this book.

—REP. DAVE WELDON

U.S. Congress

So many good, strong men start out their walk with God full of promise and great intentions. Why, then, have so many of them fallen and can't get up? Why do they feel like walking failures, duped by Delilahs of deceit over and over again? Mark Atteberry reveals the secret to a man staying strong (or getting up quickly when he falls) by taking us into the minds of both biblical and modern-day Samsons: with profoundly gleaned insight into what *not* to do. Men will love the compassionate yet confronting tone of this book, the stories that reveal where we really live, and the tragic fate that awaits the strong man who chooses to walk alone. Men, don't leave home—without reading this book. Your wives and kids will love you for it.

—BECKY FREEMAN

National Speaker and Best-selling Author

THE
SAMSON
SYNDROME

WHAT YOU CAN LEARN FROM
THE BADDEST BOY
IN THE BIBLE

MARK ATTEBERRY

W PUBLISHING GROUP

AN IMPRINT OF THOMAS NELSON

Published in Nashville, Tennessee, by Thomas Nelson.
Thomas Nelson is a registered trademark of Thomas Nelson, Inc.

Published in association with the literary agency of Alive Communications, 7680
Goddard Street, Suite 200, Colorado Springs, CO 80920.

Unless otherwise indicated, all Scripture quotations are taken from the *Holy Bible,*
New Living Translation, copyright © 1996. Used by permission of Tyndale House
Publishers, Inc. Wheaton, Illinois 60189. All rights reserved.

Scriptures marked NASB are taken from the *New American Standard Bible*®,
Copyright © The Lockman Foundation 1960, 1962, 1963, 1968, 1971, 1972, 1973,
1975, 1977, 1995. Used by permission (www.Lockman.org)

Library of Congress Cataloging-in-Publication Data

Atteberry, Mark.
    The Samson syndrome : what you can learn from the baddest boy in the
Bible / Mark Atteberry.
        p. cm.
    ISBN 0-7852-6447-7 (pbk.)
    ISBN 978-0-8499-2194-0 (rpkg.)
    1. Men—Religious life. 2. Samson (Biblical judge) 3. Masculinity—Religious
aspects—Christianity. I. Title.
    BV4528.2 .A88 2003
    248.8'42—dc21   2002152470

Printed in the United States of America
14 15 16 17 18 19 QG 6 5 4 3 2 1

———————

FOR MY FATHER, DOUG ATTEBERRY.

THANKS, DAD, FOR SHOWING ME WHAT IT MEANS
TO BE A STRONG MAN OF GOD.

———————

CONTENTS

FOREWORD

THERE WAS NOTHING SPECIAL ABOUT THE PACKAGE. IT WAS a plain manila envelope stuffed with about 250 sheets of paper. The top sheet was a cover letter asking me to read the manuscript of a new book called *The Samson Syndrome* and consider writing a blurb for the cover. The author's name was Mark Atteberry. I didn't know him but was struck by the fact that he pastors a church here in the Orlando area. It was 5:00 P.M. I had a few minutes. I decided to read a few pages and then head for home.

The next thing I knew, my phone was ringing. It was my wife, Ruth, asking when I was coming home for dinner. I looked at the clock and was stunned to realize that it was 7:20. For more than two hours I had been spellbound by this amazing book.

Why?

For one thing, it's so well written. It has that perfect balance of depth and warmth that every writer strives for. And it's loaded with wonderful stories that are both touching and humorous. I felt as if I was reading Swindoll or Lucado. I kept thinking, who is this Mark Atteberry guy and where has he been?

But there was something else. As I turned page after page I kept getting the feeling that this man had been reading my mail! Again and again I saw myself reflected in his words. They touched me deeply. They convicted me. They led me to some important, life-changing truths.

For some reason, Samson is one Bible character who hasn't gotten much attention over the years. After reading *The Samson Syndrome*, I realize what a tragedy that is. As Mark Atteberry shows us, Samson has a lot to say to the strong men of any generation.

I have always believed that the true measure of any book is changed lives. On that basis, this book is destined for greatness. It's going to change many lives, and one of them could be yours. I encourage you to read it, enjoy it, and spread the word.

Oh, and one more thing: I predict you won't be able to put this book down, so don't start reading right before dinner.

—PAT WILLIAMS
SR. VICE PRESIDENT, ORLANDO MAGIC

INTRODUCTION

PEOPLE HAVE ALWAYS BEEN FASCINATED BY DARING adventurers who live on the edge. How else do you explain the phenomenal success of James Bond 007? Ian Fleming's British superspy is the hero of over twenty films that have earned over a billion dollars worldwide. Every Bond film features dangerous villains, exotic weaponry, ingenious gadgets, fast cars, and even faster women. But it's all in a day's work for the coolest secret agent of them all, who, at last count, has saved the world twenty-three times and has yet to get his hair messed up.

This book is about a man in the Bible who was so Bondlike in his attitude and lifestyle that one wonders if he might have been part of Ian Fleming's inspiration. Samson, whose story is told in four chapters of the book of Judges, was young, strong, good-looking, cocky, courageous, and an incorrigible ladies man. He had a nose for trouble, a knack for hair-raising escapes, and more girlfriends than Radio City has Rockettes. If Samson were alive today he'd be a superstar athlete or an action-movie star. Or he'd be a Navy SEAL or a world-champion prize fighter. He'd be on the cover of *GQ* or *Sports Illustrated*. He'd be surrounded by popping flashbulbs and adoring groupies.

But he'd still be a disappointment to God.

You see, while Samson was easily the strongest man in the Bible, he was also, in many ways, the weakest. He was hand-picked by a gracious God to lead his people, the Israelites, in a revolt against the dreaded Philistines, who had been oppressing them without resistance for forty years. And talk about gifts! No one in Scripture could match Samson for sheer talent and potential. But rather than developing into a thrilling saga of faith and patriotism, Samson's story degenerates quickly into a tawdry soap opera. Oh yes, there are flashes of greatness, brief moments when we catch little glimpses of the hero God intended for him to be. But for the most part, Samson was a selfish, shallow-minded playboy who squandered his talents.

Perhaps this is why Samson is largely ignored in print. Very few books about him exist. To most Christians he is merely "the guy who fooled around with Delilah" or "that strong dude with the long hair." We apparently think he has little to say to the modern believer. We prefer instead to focus our attention on more positive, politically correct characters and expound end-lessly on their "secrets of success."

But let me ask you a question.

Would God have devoted a whopping four chapters (ninety-six verses) of His precious Word to Samson's story if it *didn't* contain a powerful message for His people?

Of course not.

That's why I think it's high time we rediscovered Samson. I believe this Bible bad boy has been trying to tell us something for years. Something important. And I believe his message is needed now more than ever.

SAMSON'S MESSAGE

Very simply, I believe Samson teaches us why strong men fail.

Think about it.

Strong, talented, godly men should be the pillars of our homes, churches, and communities. But too often they aren't. The pages of history are filled with heartbreaking stories of strong, godly men who disgraced themselves by falling into sin. For example, King David of Israel, the mighty warrior and man after God's own heart, wandered through a year-long period of darkness in which he stole another man's wife and orchestrated a murder plot that had enough intrigue to fill an Alfred Hitchcock double feature. And what about all the fallen heroes in our day? Off the top of your head, you could probably name at least a half-dozen strong men of good reputation who have suffered moral failure and public disgrace. From professional athletes to entertainers to business executives to clergymen, we're constantly hearing the gory details of how a good boy turned bad.

But it's not just celebrities and public figures who stumble. It's us too. The guys who may not be famous, but nonetheless are raising the children, leading the churches, and running the businesses of America.

I believe *all* men stand to benefit from Samson's message, even those who may not at this moment be teetering on the edge of some great moral abyss. I also believe that the women who love strong men can gain some valuable insights from Samson's experiences. After all, much of the biblical narrative focuses on his relationships and interactions with females. There is no character in the Bible that offers a woman keener insights into the male psyche.

However, there is a certain type of man who should find Samson's message especially helpful.

Perhaps, like Samson, you've been richly blessed and gifted by God. You sense his call on your life and you know he has important work for you to do. You've got a responsible job and people look up to you. You've got a great wife and beautiful kids and you've already tasted enough success to know the sky's the limit.   But something is wrong.

Your friends don't see it. Even your wife might be overlooking the subtle signs. But it's happening. You can feel yourself drifting. For some reason, you're just not as passionate about the things of God as you used to be. And your marriage, though it isn't all that bad, doesn't satisfy you the way it used to. Perhaps at times you even feel drawn to things that you know should be off limits for a person of faith. Maybe you've even begun to dabble in some of those things (secretly, of course) and can feel the grip of sin tightening on your life. You couldn't begin to explain why you're in trouble, you just know you are. And now you're wondering—and are perhaps terrified of where it will all end.

Well, friend, it's to you that Samson speaks the loudest.

THE SAMSON SYNDROME

After almost thirty years in the preaching ministry, and with much of that time spent working closely with strong men of faith, I have come to believe in what I call *The Samson Syndrome*. *The Samson Syndrome* is a set of twelve tendencies revealed in the biblical account of Samson's life that clearly contributed to his erratic behavior, his spiritual decline, and ultimately, his failure as a deliverer of God's people. These tendencies are common to men of strength in every generation. They represent the unique challenges that strong men will always face. A man may have to contend with one of them or all twelve, but no man will totally escape their influence. Simply put, these tendencies are the reasons why strong men fail.

What I'll do in this book is explain each tendency and show why it is often a problem for strong men. Then I'll offer some specific, positive suggestions on how you can overcome it. I'll warn you now that this book will take us into some dark territory. Samson's trail will lead us to some topics that aren't often discussed around the dinner table. But we'll view them all through the lens of Scripture, we'll lighten up and have a few laughs along the way, and in the end, I believe we'll all be better equipped to stand firm in our faith, to fulfill our God-given potential, and even to exceed our loftiest aspirations.

So I invite you to keep reading and join me on a fascinating journey back to a time of danger and intrigue. Let's walk the dusty roads of Israel. Let's step into the teeming marketplaces and onto the bloody battlefields of that ancient, mysterious land. Let's listen in on the secret conversations of deadly enemies and the pillow talk of illicit lovers. Let's witness the weakness of man in all its shame and the power of God in all its glory. And through it all, let's learn how to be faithful and to live with honor before God so that we might never have to stand before Him and explain why we didn't accomplish the things He called us to do.

HISTORICAL NOTE

AT THE BEGINNING OF JUDGES 13 WE FIND GOD FED up with his people. He was so disgusted with their disobedience that he decided to hand them over to the Philistines. The idea was that the crack of a whip across their backs might help them see the error of their ways. But it didn't work. Not only did they accept slavery as a way of life, their lack of repentance suggests that they actually grew content with it. That they didn't cry out to God is amazing, but not half as amazing as the fact that God decided to deliver them anyway. In what could only be described as a phenomenal act of grace, God decided to raise up a strong man to lead His unrepentant people out of bondage.

That man was Samson.

His godly parents knew from the beginning that he had been handpicked by God and did their best to raise him according to the instructions they received from an angel of the Lord (13:5). As far as we know, the first few years of Samson's life were relatively uneventful. The Bible says God blessed him as he grew up (13:24), no doubt both physically and spiritually.

But like so many people today, Samson appears to have been negatively influenced by the culture in which he lived. Judges 17:6 says that in those days the people "did whatever seemed right in their own eyes." God intended for Samson to elevate that mind-set, but instead he adopted it. By the time he was twenty he had already slipped into some very dangerous behavior patterns.

Samson never attempted to rally his countrymen in an organized attempt to overthrow the Philistines. If he had, we know he would have been successful, for God had already approved the idea and was apparently just waiting to bless the effort (13:5). No doubt Samson's reluctance was due in part to his romantic entanglements with various Philistine women. He did conduct a highly successful guerilla campaign against certain Philistines who aroused his anger, but those raids and ambushes were designed only to satisfy his lust for revenge and never came close to liberating his people.

Samson's name, which means "sunny," was well chosen by his parents. They knew he was supposed to be a bright ray of hope bursting through the dismal existence that his people were enduring. However, the name "cloudy" would have been more appropriate because he never delivered on his potential. In fact, his rare moments of zeal and mind-boggling feats of strength only serve to magnify his failures because they show us how different things could have been.

ONE

STRONG MEN TEND TO DISREGARD BOUNDARIES

Mickey Mantle's carousing knew no limits. I'd say he easily took five years off of his life.

—WHITEY FORD

The gateway to life is small, and the road is narrow.

—JESUS CHRIST (MATTHEW 7:14)

BOUNDARIES. FROM DAY ONE WE HAVE TO CONTEND with them.

Moments after your birth you were wrapped in a blanket and put into a bed that looked something like a fish tank on wheels. Then when you got home, your parents put you in a bed that had bars like a jail cell. And when it was time to play, they dropped you into something called a "playpen." At first these enclosures were of no concern. But as your motor skills developed and your mobility increased, you began to feel quite restricted.

And then one day it hit you: You were being tricked.

They called it a *playpen* to make it sound enticing. They filled it with your favorite toys and they always talked mushy baby talk when they stuck you in it. But suddenly you knew. You saw the truth as clearly as if it were written on the wall in crayon: You were being held prisoner. They could call the devilish contraption anything they wanted, but a cage by any other name is still a cage.

And that's when you rebelled. Big time. At the top of your lungs. With some kicking and tears thrown in for good measure. And you didn't stop until somebody came and liberated you.

But your victory was short-lived, for there were more boundaries in your future.

"Go to your room."

"Sit in that chair until I say you can get up."

"It's your bedtime."

"If you ever say that again, I'll wash your mouth out with soap!"

"Change the channel. You're not watching that garbage!"

"Be home by eleven."

"No, you can't get a tattoo."

If you were like most kids, you couldn't wait to turn eighteen. You dreamed of a life without parental authority. No more boundaries. No more restrictions. Finally, after years of oppression, you would be free to live your life the way you saw fit. But it was a pipe dream.

> NO MATTER HOW OLD YOU ARE AS YOU READ THIS BOOK, YOU CAN STILL COUNT NUMEROUS BOUNDARIES THAT HEM YOU IN.

No matter how old you are as you read this book, you can still count numerous boundaries that hem you in. If it's not the speed-limit signs you pass on your way to work, it's your doctor's orders to stay away from all your favorite foods. Yes, boundaries are a fact of life. And though we spend our lives grousing about them and trying to stretch them as far as possible, we must admit that we wouldn't last long without them. With a few exceptions, boundaries are designed to keep us on track and out of trouble.

That's why God laid out some specific boundaries for Samson at the very beginning of his life. Check out these specific instructions that an angel of the Lord gave to Samson's mother: "You will become pregnant and give birth to a son, and his hair must never be cut. For he will be dedicated to God as a Nazirite from birth. He will rescue Israel from the Philistines" (Judg. 13:5).

Numbers 6 gives a detailed description of the Nazirite vow. It was generally taken voluntarily for a period of thirty or sixty days by people who had a desire for a deeper, more intimate connection with God. During this time they were to observe some very specific boundaries. They had to stay away from things that were *unwise* (strong drink), *unclean* (dead bodies), and *unnecessary* (the cutting of hair). It was a vow that required great devotion and attention to detail, and God was insisting that Samson live under it, not for a month or two, but for his entire life.

Seems oppressive, doesn't it? Sounds like God was determined not to let Samson have any fun at all. But there was more to it than that.

You see, God made Samson and fully understood his personality. As a strong "alpha male," he would be gutsy and bodacious. Daring and impulsive. Reckless and carefree. Of course, these were the qualities that would serve him well as a military commander leading an insurrection against the Philistines. But they were also the traits that could get him into trouble spiritually and lead him far from God. That's why God placed him under the Nazirite vow. It was His way of keeping Samson from spinning out of control.

Unfortunately, it didn't work. As we will see throughout this book, Samson only respected God's boundaries when it suited him. The rest of the time he did whatever he wanted. And he wasn't afraid of getting into trouble because he believed his great strength would bail him out of any predicament he might get into.

Sound familiar?

Maybe you know a guy like that.

Maybe you *are* a guy like that.

Maybe you're a guy who, like Samson, was taught as a child to respect God's law. You went to church every Sunday, memorized the Ten Commandments, starred in numerous Sunday-school productions, and had every little old lady in the church thinking you were just the cutest thing they'd ever seen. But at some point—possibly during your high-school or college years—those Commandments started feeling a little restrictive, like a suit that's a couple of sizes too small. You found that you couldn't run with the fun crowd and be a staunch Ten-Commandments guy at the same time, so you started making a few compromises. Nothing serious. Just a little fooling around. After all, boys will be boys.

That's exactly how it started with Samson. He didn't wake up one day and suddenly decide to trash his Nazirite vow. Instead, he slipped gradually into a life of disobedience by making a series of small compromises. And every time he did, you can be sure he was relying on his great strength to be his safety net. "I can handle it" was his motto.

Is it yours?

What are you "handling" right now? Are there some fences in your life that have been trampled by your desire for money, power, or pleasure? Are there some things you're doing that you know God doesn't approve of? Some things that you're having to hide? Some things that would horrify your wife and children, not to mention those little old ladies who adored you as a child?

Strong men who have great confidence in their ability to "handle things" often disregard boundaries. But they do so at great risk. Samson's tragic story reveals two bad things that will eventually happen if you continually disregard God's boundaries.

YOU WILL BE SHACKLED

On July 6, 1999, twenty-seven-year-old Daniel Dukes went to SeaWorld here in Orlando. He gave every appearance of being an ordinary tourist, but he wasn't. At closing time, as all the other guests were leaving the park, he ducked into a hiding place and stayed put until the park was empty. Then, sometime during the night, he made his way to the pool where a five-ton killer whale named Tillicum was being kept. He stripped down to his swimming trunks, folded his clothes neatly, and jumped in.

Nobody knows for sure what happened next. Some experts believe the whale may have been startled by the man's sudden appearance. In his fear, he may have dived suddenly, creating a vortex that pulled the man under and rendered him helpless. Others believe it's more likely that the whale thought the man was a toy and dragged him around the pool for fun, keeping him underwater until he drowned. Either way, Dukes's body was found the next morning draped over Tillicum's back.

When I first heard that story on the news I thought it was a perfect picture of the consequences of sin. We climb over fences, not to wreak havoc and destruction, but just to have a little fun. The problem is, we underestimate the danger. We intend to stay only a little while, but sin grabs us in its teeth and refuses to let go.

Samson is a case in point. His intention was never to fight against God. He was just a fun-loving guy out looking for a good time. Like so many strong men today, he didn't think his sin was any big deal. But it's clear as you read his story that the older he got, the more sin held him in its grip. Think about the night he was in bed with a prostitute while a band of Philistine soldiers was surrounding her house (Judg. 16:1–3). Somehow he managed to slip out under the cover of darkness in a James Bond–like escape. But even that close call wasn't enough to bring him to his senses. By then he was hopelessly shackled.

Today our countless drug and alcohol rehab centers are vivid proof that people are still being shackled by sin. And that's not to mention all the therapists and counselors who spend eight hours a day trying to help their patients sort through their sin-induced problems. I daresay that none of those patients ever intended to become so tangled up and overwhelmed, but it happened because they failed to recognize the addictive and destructive nature of sin. It will reduce even the strongest men to pathetic buffoons.

At the end of Samson's life we see him doing hard labor in a Philistine prison. He's blind and exhausted, staggering around and bumping into things, falling down and causing hysterical laughter among his captors. I pray that every man who reads this book will close his eyes and let that image sink in. It is perhaps the best picture we have in all the Bible of the destructive power of sin.

I'll say it as simply as I can. If you've been willfully climbing over God's boundaries to indulge in sin, you must stop it. If you don't, you could wake up someday and, like Samson, find that you've been shackled.

But that's not all.

YOU WILL BE SHAMED

Samson's shame reached its peak when we see him blind and bound, stumbling and bumbling to the delight of his enemies. But the Bible contains other equally tragic stories about strong men who disregarded God's boundaries and suffered public shame as a result.

David's is perhaps the most familiar.

You remember how he flexed his political muscle and had the gorgeous Bathsheba brought to his bedroom. Apparently, he wasn't anticipating anything more than a one-night stand. His idea was to use her and lose her. But when she turned up pregnant, the need for damage control became paramount, as it always does with powerful politicians. It would have been nice if he'd simply repented and thrown himself on the mercy of the Lord, but because he was now *shackled* by sin (remember, he had a house full of wives), that option was never considered. Instead, he formulated a detailed plan to cover his tracks, which ultimately involved eliminating Bathsheba's husband. It worked, and in no time she had moved into the palace and was picking out draperies. It was all very neat and tidy, except for one thing: God had been watching David's every move.

You'll recall how God sent Nathan to confront David. The message he brought is one that should send chills down your spine if you're a man who dabbles in secret sin: "Because of what you have done, I, the LORD, will cause your own household to rebel against you. I will give your wives to another man, and he will go to bed with them in public view. *You did it secretly, but I will do this to you openly in the sight of all Israel"* (2 Sam. 12:11–12, author's emphasis).

God has a way of bringing the secret sins of strong men out into the open. Just ask Bill Clinton. Or Jesse Jackson. Or any one of a million other humiliated men who thought they were sly and sneaky enough to step over God's boundaries and get away with it.

> IF YOU'VE TRAMPLED GOD'S FENCES AND ARE PARTAKING OF THINGS THAT HE HAS SAID ARE OFF LIMITS, YOU NEED TO UNDERSTAND THAT YOU ARE IN GRAVE DANGER OF BEING SHAMED.

Right now, if you've trampled God's fences and are partaking of things that he has said are off limits, you need to understand that you are in grave danger of being shamed. You have set yourself in opposition to almighty God and are just asking to be publicly broken and humiliated. Zephaniah 1:12 says, "I will search with lanterns in Jerusalem's darkest corners to find and punish those who sit contented in their sins, indifferent to the LORD, thinking he will do nothing at all to them." My friend, if that verse doesn't shake you out of your moral complacency, I fear that nothing ever will.

But if it does . . . if it helps you realize that you need to make some changes in the way you've been living, let me offer you a simple plan of action.

YOU CAN BE SPARED

Four simple steps will ensure that you don't have to endure the shackles and the shame a wandering life always seems to bring.

First, REMEMBER the joy of living within God's boundaries. It's entirely possible that you've been living outside them for so long that you've forgotten how good it feels to be on the inside.

A man named Jerry made this discovery about himself when he pulled an innocent-looking envelope out of his mailbox. He opened it and removed an invitation to the twenty-year reunion of his Bible-college graduating class. He'd graduated from the school and spent three years in youth ministry before losing his job during a bitter church split. Frustrated and disillusioned, he left the ministry and pursued a career as a police officer. He was good at the job and earned numerous awards and citations. But the environment took a toll on his commitment to the Lord. Within a year, he had dropped out of church, was hanging out after hours at a bar near his precinct station, and was picking up the language of the street. He also got married and divorced twice within a five-year period and fathered a son that he hardly ever saw.

But the invitation stopped him cold.

On the front of the card was a picture of his graduating class. There he was: third row, fourth from the left. Standing right next to the guy who had been his roommate and best friend. Two rows in front of the preacher's daughter he'd been madly in love with during his junior year. Looking at himself standing among his old friends, he noticed that they were all grinning from ear to ear. Suddenly, he felt a swirl of emotion. More than nostalgia, it was a rush of regret. He'd changed so much since then, and not for the better. Though successful in the eyes of the world, he had lost virtually all of what had once given his life meaning and purpose. Staring at his own smiling face in the picture, he wondered how many years it had been since he'd been *that* happy.

The good news is that Jerry picked up the phone that very day and called his old roommate. He ended up attending the reunion and reconnecting with some of his old friends. It was a small step, but the first step in a long journey back to his first love and to the happiness he'd all but forgotten.

One of the blessings of being in the preaching ministry is that I get to meet a lot of Jerrys, a lot of returning prodigals who always remind me that life is better inside God's boundaries. Recently a wandering prodigal came home during one of our worship services. He squeezed me so tight he just about broke my ribs. As he sobbed on my shoulder he kept saying over and over, "It's so good to be home . . . so good to be home . . . so good to be home . . ." Every time something like that happens I say to myself, "Mark, there's no reason for you to ever go wandering off. No matter what the world tries to tell you, life really is better on the inside."

Maybe this would be a good time for you to look back and remember.

Second, RENOUNCE any activity that has lured you outside God's boundaries in the past. I love football, but I've never quite figured out what it is about Monday night that makes any game seem like a miniature Super Bowl. Even when the two worst teams in the league are matched up, all the rowdies still get together, order in mountains of pizza and beer, and hoot and holler like there's no tomorrow.

In one neighborhood, Andy was the self-proclaimed King of Monday Night. His house was *the* place to be when ol' Hank Jr. shouted, "Are you ready for some football?" He had the two most desired Monday night amenities: a big screen TV and an oversized refrigerator. And he lacked the one most undesired

Monday night encumbrance: a wife. Yes sir, Andy's place was Monday night heaven.

Until he went and ruined everything by becoming a Christian.

Ruined everything for his buddies, that is, because, with his new commitment to the Lord came a few new rules, such as "No booze." When Andy informed his rowdy friends that they would now be drinking Pepsi on Monday nights, they groaned as if he had said, "Castor Oil."

Not surprisingly, the King of Monday Night was dethroned. His usual crowd of twelve dwindled to six, to four, and then to nothing. But if you ask Andy, he'll tell you that he gained more than he lost.

It will sound extreme to some, but if you are to avoid the Samson Syndrome, there must be nothing in your life—no person, no possession, no activity—that you value more than your relationship with God. If there's *anything* in your life that lures you outside God's boundaries, kiss it good-bye.

Third, REBUILD the fences you've trampled. A fence is anything that keeps you from straying. It might be the disciplines of prayer, Bible study, or corporate worship that you abandoned somewhere along the way. It might be a relationship with a strong Christian that you allowed to wither and die. Or it might be some ministry or service project that kept you from having too much free time on your hands.

I remember years ago a man in our church came to me and volunteered to teach a Sunday-school class. I thought he must be delirious. After all, nobody *ever* volunteers to teach a Sunday-school class. Halley's Comet splits the eastern sky with greater regularity. But there he was, standing right in front of me, actually saying the words.

When I asked him why, he stopped me cold with his answer.

He said, "I used to teach a long time ago, and I've come to realize that I'm a much better Christian when I'm teaching Sunday school."

You see, for him, teaching Sunday school was a fence that helped keep him inside God's boundaries. It kept his nose in the Word, gave him a sense of purpose, and occupied some of his free time with a worthwhile endeavor.

Are there some fences in your life that have been trampled or that have fallen into disrepair? If so, you need to rebuild them. You need to get back to the people, places, and things that keep you in the will of God.

And finally, REJOICE in the mercy and grace of a forgiving God. Forgiveness can be pretty hard to come by in this world. Take the odd case of Jefferson Davis, for example. He was the president of the Confederacy, and before the Civil War, had been a congressman, senator, and a member of the president's Cabinet. But after the war he was considered a traitor. His citizenship was revoked and he was thrown into prison for two years. It wasn't until October 17, 1978—a full eighty-nine years after his death—that Jefferson Davis was officially "forgiven" by the United States government and had his citizenship restored.

If you've strayed outside God's boundaries, and especially if your straying has hurt some people, they may find it just as hard to forgive you as our government did Jefferson Davis. Countless men have been rejected by their families and friends, or have lost their careers because of their sins. But the promise of Scripture is that God, like the prodigal son's father, is full of mercy and grace and stands ready to welcome us home when we come in genuine repentance. First John 1:9 says, "If we confess our sins to him, he is faithful and just to forgive us and to cleanse us from every wrong."

One of the more encouraging aspects of Samson's story is that every time he turned to God, even if his motivations were somewhat skewed, God was there for him. And you can be sure He'll be there for you too. Jesus said, "Come to me, *all of you* who are weary and carry heavy burdens, and I will give you rest" (Matt. 11:28, author's emphasis).

Are there any more beautiful words in Scripture?

TWO

STRONG MEN TEND TO STRUGGLE WITH LUST

Love is the answer. But while you're waiting for the answer, sex raises some pretty good questions.

—WOODY ALLEN

So put to death the sinful, earthly things lurking within you. Have nothing to do with sexual sin, impurity, lust, and shameful desires.

—PAUL THE APOSTLE (COLOSSIANS 3:5)

WHEN WE FIRST MEET SAMSON AT THE BEGINNING of Judges 14, he's walking the streets of the Philistine village of Timnah, which was approximately six miles from his home in Zorah. At about twenty years of age, we'd like to believe he was finally preparing to assume his role as the leader of God's people. We'd like to think he was putting the final touches on a plan to rally his Israelite brothers against the Philistines. We'd like to think he entered enemy territory to gather intelligence.

However, it appears he was only there to check out the babes.

Picture him walking up and down the streets of Timnah, winking and smiling at every girl he passed. Of course, some were too unattractive or too married to warrant anything more than a casual glance. But eventually he spotted one that rang his chimes. We're not told her name or anything else about her, only that Samson liked her looks, wanted her, and was determined to have her at any cost.

And so began Samson's lifelong battle with lust.

It's not surprising that he fought such a battle because, from Samson to Bill Clinton, it's the men of power and influence in every culture that are considered to be sexy. No doubt you've seen a gorgeous young woman in her twenties hanging on the arm of a below- average-looking middle-aged man, and wondered, "What in the world does she see in him?" To you and me it makes no sense, but survey after survey indicates that women are more attracted to power and influence than looks, education, talent, or even character. Even our children's fairy tales reinforce the notion. Remember how Cinderella's ugly sisters were so desperate to marry into the royal family that they were willing to painfully cram their oversized feet into a tiny glass slipper?

> WHEN YOU'VE BEEN WIRED BY YOUR CREATOR TO LOVE SEX . . . AND ARE CONSIDERED TO BE A PRIZE "CATCH" BY CERTAIN FLIRTATIOUS MEMBERS OF THE OPPOSITE SEX, THAT CAN BE A PRESCRIPTION FOR TROUBLE.

Of course, I'm not suggesting that all men of strength struggle with lust. Many don't. And of course, weak men often face this battle too. But the Samson Syndrome is about tendencies, and let's face it, guys. When you've been wired by your Creator to love sex, are living in a sexually permissive culture, are used to getting what you want, and are considered to be a prize "catch" by certain flirtatious members of the opposite sex, that can be a prescription for trouble.

To me, the hardest part of any discussion about lust is simply trying to define it. Jesus said, "Anyone who even looks at a woman with lust in his eye has already committed adultery with her in his heart" (Matthew 5:28). The reason that's such a scary verse is because there's so much uncertainty about what it means to look at a woman with lust in your eye.

The typical man reads that verse and immediately pictures a beautiful woman. Maybe someone he works with or someone he just saw at the mall. Then he remembers how he checked her out. Not that he whistled or drooled or barked like a dog, but he knows he gave her the once-over—discreetly, of course—and had a thought or two pass through his mind that had nothing to do with last week's Sunday-school lesson. And then he wonders . . .

Was I lusting?

Am I an adulterer?

Do I need to repent?

Is there something wrong with me?

It's unfortunate that no one has ever come up with a definition of lust that everybody can agree on. We know it has to do with sex, it's a mind thing, and it's bad. But where does normal sexual desire end and lust begin? As one of my friends said, "If you stand up and preach about lying, I know exactly what you're talking about and I know if I'm guilty. But if you start talking about lust, all of a sudden I'm not sure where I stand."

We may never come up with a definition of lust that satisfies everybody, but I do believe we can understand it. The key is to see it in action, to observe the behavior of someone who is obviously being driven by lust.

Enter Samson.

If you look closely at his behavior, you'll see that lust causes a person to make two grave mistakes.

LUST CAUSES A PERSON TO IGNORE SPIRITUAL CONSIDERATIONS

I heard about a notorious playboy who was out on his first date with an attractive but principled young woman. She sensed that he had an eye for the ladies, so she asked him a pointed question. "Do women always run through your mind?" He winked and flashed a devilish grin. "Yes," he said. "They know better than to walk."

I wouldn't want to know what images were running through Samson's mind as he prowled the streets of Timnah, ogling the young Philistine women. We know he wasn't whistling praise choruses or reciting the Ten Commandments, because when his parents did try to raise the issue of the girl's spiritual heritage, Samson reacted harshly, nipping the discussion in the bud. In essence, he said, "Who cares if she's a pagan? She's *hot* and that's all I care about!" There was absolutely no consideration of the spiritual ramifications of romancing the girl.

The next time you feel a twinge of sexual desire toward someone or something illicit, stop and remind yourself of a simple but important truth that Samson obviously forgot: that the primary difference between a man and an animal is that a man has the ability to act according to reason rather than instinct.

Let those two words settle in your mind.

Reason and *instinct*.

A man has the ability to reason his way through a situation, weighing the pros and cons, evaluating the risks and rewards, and considering the spiritual ramifications, while animals act entirely according to instinct. This means that when you throw reason to the wind and act solely according to the impulses of your flesh, you become no different than your dog or the old tomcat that prowls the alley behind your house.

Perhaps you're thinking, *Yes, but sex is an inherently primal act, isn't it? Don't we all become animals to some extent when we enter the sexual arena?*

I can certainly see why a person might believe that. Our culture has done everything it can to animalize sex. Not long ago I happened to be channel surfing and stumbled across one of the late-afternoon cable talk shows. The topic had something to do with kinky sex, and a couple was being interviewed. He looked like any forty-year-old man you might see walking down the street, but she was bound in chains like a wild animal. She even had an iron collar around her neck with a leash attached to it.

> WHEN YOU THROW REASON TO THE WIND AND ACT SOLELY ACCORDING TO THE IMPULSES OF YOUR FLESH, YOU BECOME NO DIFFERENT THAN YOUR DOG OR THE OLD TOMCAT THAT PROWLS THE ALLEY BEHIND YOUR HOUSE.

Because of the animalization of sex in our culture, most people don't realize that the human sex act was designed by God to be very different from the animal sex act.

Consider the following facts.

First, humans are the only creatures on earth that are anatomically designed for face-to-face mating. Virtually all of the erogenous zones of the human body are on the front and create a greater potential for pleasure when brought together in a "whole-body" experience. Face-to-face mating puts the arms and hands in the perfect position to caress and embrace, and encourages communication by allowing the man and woman to look into each other's eyes and whisper into each other's ears. This is not to suggest that other sexual positions are sinful, simply that men and women were designed to make face-to-face mating easy and pleasurable.

Animals, on the other hand, normally practice dorsal-ventral (front to back) mating and do not have a "whole-body" experience. Even on rare occasions when some primates stumble onto the face-to-face position by accident, they still only make brief contact in the genital area.

Second, the human female is the only female that can have an orgasm. This means that a woman can derive as much pleasure from the sex act as her male partner, giving them yet another bonding experience. Mutual pleasure also means that both the man and the woman will desire sex and will enjoy it at various times of their own choosing as they enhance their relationship.

YOU WERE INTENDED TO EXPERIENCE SOMETHING MORE THAN THE EMPTY, ROBOTIC MATING RITUALS OF THE ANIMAL KINGDOM.

Animals, on the other hand, do not have a relationship to enhance. They are motivated to mate by a cycle of heat and ovulation. They are driven by seasonal impulses rather than a desire for pleasure or interaction with the opposite sex.

Third, humans are the only creatures on earth that are capable of understanding and enjoying romance. Many animal species have instinctive rituals that indicate a readiness for sex, but this is not to be confused with romance. Only humans enjoy candlelight dinners, walks in the moonlight, love letters, poems, romantic music, back rubs, and of course, prolonged and passionate kissing.

Put it all together and the conclusion is unmistakable: God intended for human sex to be *different* from animal sex. He intended for it to have a higher purpose than mere procreation. He intended for it to be a means of personal interaction and relationship building, something that would elevate and enhance the marriage relationship. In other words, He intended for it to have a *spiritual* dimension.

The very thing lust causes you to ignore.

My friend, I challenge you to be different from the world, to embrace your sexuality in a manner worthy of the exalted position God has given you in His creation. Remember, you were created "a little lower than God" (Ps. 8:5). You were intended to experience something more than the empty, robotic mating rituals of the animal kingdom. You were designed to *make love* in all its facets and dimensions and to know an intimacy that reaches all the way to your soul.

But there's another grave mistake lust causes a person to make.

LUST CAUSES A PERSON TO IGNORE GOD'S PLAN

The Bible makes it clear that lust made an early appearance on the stage of history:

"When the human population began to grow rapidly on the earth, the sons of God saw the beautiful women of the human race and took any they wanted as their wives" (Gen. 6:1–2).

Those words are very hard to interpret because, as Stuart Briscoe says, we know what the "sons of God" were doing; we just don't know for certain who they were. Two theories have been proposed.

First, they were fallen angels who came to earth to have sex with humans. Of course, many dismiss such a notion as preposterous, but four facts should be carefully considered. First, the language being used would actually accommodate such an interpretation. Second, Genesis 6:4 says that the offspring produced by this union possessed some superhuman qualities. Third, Jude 6 says that there was indeed a time when angels left the place where they belonged. And fourth, there is a horrifying scene in Genesis 19 where men were all set to have sex with angels, and apparently would have if Lot hadn't intervened.

The second view is less controversial and more acceptable to most people. *The "sons of God" were the descendants of Seth.* That is, men of righteous lineage who knew God and practiced religion.

My purpose here is not to take a stand on either of these views because it isn't necessary. No matter who the "sons of God" were, the essential truth of the passage comes shining through. It's simply that lust had confused and distracted righteous beings (whether they were men or angels) and caused them to pursue unwholesome activities that were foreign to the plan and purpose of God.

The same thing happened to Samson.

He was supposed to be plotting the demise of the Philistines, but instead he was planning a wedding. Imagine getting measured for a tux when you're supposed to be planning an attack against your bride's family! And the tragic truth is that he never did fulfill God's plan. Sure, he carried on a personal feud with the Philistines throughout his life and killed an impressive number of them, but he was so distracted by his constant pursuit of sexual gratification that he never became the Moseslike deliverer that God intended for him to be.

What about you?

Are you also distracted by your interest in sex?

Would you be forced to admit that you spend a good bit of time trying to satisfy your desires in ways that you'd never want anyone to know about?

Do you read trashy novels?

Do you spend time in Internet chat rooms flirting with total strangers?

Do you watch adult movies when you're home alone?

Do you visit strip clubs and adult bookstores when you're out of town?

Do you masturbate regularly?

Do you concoct lies and excuses to cover up these activities?

Do you have a secret intimate relationship with someone?

Do you find ways to excuse behavior that you know in your heart is inexcusable?

If your answer is "Yes" to any of these questions, then my friend, you have strayed far from where God wants you to be. It doesn't matter if you still give some of your time and energy to his service. *Any* amount of time invested in the pursuits listed above is an indication that you have lost sight of God's plan for your life. Lust is controlling you, and if you don't take action to correct the problem, it will ruin your life.

A PLAN OF ACTION

Let me suggest four steps that will help you bring your sexual desires under control.

First, get right. Recently, there was a story in the news about a man with a history of sex offenses who castrated himself with a kitchen knife in a desperate attempt to gain control over his desires. Sadly, he was focused on the wrong organ. The Bible teaches that it's the heart we need to be concerned about. Proverbs 4:23 says, "Above all else, guard your heart, for it affects everything you do."

Getting right is always an "inside-out" process. A friend of mine who restores old cars in his spare time bought a junker not long ago. And what do you think was the first thing he did? You think he took it down to the body shop and gave it a spiffy new paint job? No way. The first thing he did was raise the hood and tear into the engine. In his words, "She ain't worth paintin' if she don't run."

The process of getting right always begins "under the hood." That means getting your heart right with God before you take any other steps. You need to go to your knees and confess your sin. All of it. Don't beat around the bush or try to dress it up in pretty language. Just call it what it is and ask for God's forgiveness. Then make up your mind that you're going to do whatever it takes to stay on the straight and narrow.

Second, get away. Paul said to Timothy, "Run from anything that stimulates youthful lust" (2 Tim. 2:22). In other words, you must cut yourself off from anything that makes it easy for you to abandon your new commitment to purity.

When Julius Caesar invaded Britain, he landed his ships and unloaded his men and supplies. Then, under the cover of darkness, he sent a small team of men back out into the bay to set the ships on fire. As they sank, Caesar's men realized that retreat was no longer an option, and with that realization, their chances of success increased. You see, when we know that turning back isn't an option, we tend to put everything we have into going forward.

What are the ships you need to sink?

Maybe your "fleet" consists of videos or magazines you keep hidden away.

Or those premium movie channels you pay extra for.

Or the job that continually puts you in hotel rooms all alone and far from home. (Radical? Yes. But maybe necessary.)

Or that coworker you've been flirting with at the office.

If you're serious about bringing your sexual desires and involvements under control, you simply must start sinking some ships. You will fail if you don't.

Third, get help. Human willpower is an incredible thing. I was reminded of that recently as I was watching an episode of *Survivor.* The gutsy—or should I say, crazy—contestants were eating live worms, raw cow brains, and a few other things that are too disgusting to mention, all for the chance to win a million dollars. You might think that if a person could muster the willpower to do that, he would be able to do anything.

But that's not true.

The problem is that for some men, lust is more than just a juvenile lack of self-discipline. Instead, it's an addiction that's just as real as any drug or alcohol problem. In fact, by some estimates, as many as one out of every ten men is addicted to sex. These men may well hate themselves for their shameful indulgences. They may have promised themselves and God a thousand times that they would quit, only to fall back into the same behavior a few days (or hours) later. Some guys even see their careers and most precious relationships deteriorating because of their conduct, but still can't find the strength to quit.

Sound familiar? If so, you're going to have to get some help. I don't care how fired up you are right now to finally defeat this sin. Eventually, the emotion will subside and the desire will come creeping back in. Satan will see to it.

Fortunately, there are some excellent organizations and counselors that have proven effective in dealing with sexual addiction. You need to do some research, find one that works for you logistically, and then stick with it. Don't just go to a session or two and declare yourself healed. Make up your mind that it's going to be a long haul. Indeed, a lifelong battle.

Fourth, get busy. The elimination of sexual habits is going to open up pockets of time in your daily routine that will need to be filled. A college student named James found this out when he decided to take dead aim on his Internet addiction. He'd reached the point at which he was spending several hours every evening surfing erotic chat rooms and porn sites. Most days he was on-line from just after dinner until two or three in the morning. As a result, in addition to the guilt he was feeling, he could barely stay awake in class and once almost fell asleep while driving his car. After several failed attempts to break the habit through sheer willpower, James made a smart move at the suggestion of his minister. He got a second job. Not because he needed the money, but because he needed something to do during those evening hours when he was home alone.

Jesus would have approved of such a move. In fact, He once told a story about an evil spirit that left a man and wandered in the desert searching for rest. Finding none, it returned to the same man and found that his life was empty. So it recruited seven more evil spirits, each more evil than itself, and moved back in (Matt. 12:43–44). If only the man had gotten busy and filled that void in his life, the evil spirit would have left him alone.

If you're a strong man who struggles with lust, I'm sure you've become very good at covering your tracks. From finding the perfect hiding place for your disks and magazines to inventing excuses your spouse will believe, you've no doubt invested a lot of energy in keeping your sin a secret. On some level you're probably proud of yourself for being so creative.

But you're not happy.

Every day you live, not just with shame and guilt, but with the knowledge that one little slipup could ruin everything. You may be a church leader, a teacher, a CEO, an elected official, or a respected family man. You may have a spouse, children, parents, or employees who would be devastated if your secret were exposed. You've probably had nightmares about it. You've probably also had close calls, moments when you were almost caught and felt hot waves of panic burning your throat and chest.

Honestly, why would you want to go on living this way?

Doesn't the idea of a guilt-free, shame-free, deception-free life sound nice?

Wouldn't you like to live every day without the fear of being ruined?

Wouldn't you like to be able to give your spouse a kiss that isn't also a lie?

Wouldn't you like to go to church next Sunday without feeling like a hypocrite?

Read these words of David carefully:

> When I refused to confess my sin, I was weak and miserable, and I groaned all day long. Day and night your hand of discipline was heavy on me. My strength evaporated like water in the summer heat . . . Finally, I confessed all my sins

to you and stopped trying to hide them. I said to myself, "I will confess my rebellion to the LORD." And you forgave me! All my guilt is gone. (Ps. 32:3–5)

All my guilt is gone.
Do you realize that those words could be *your* words?
Think about it.
No more hiding.
No more pretending.
No more fear.
No more smiling as if you're on your way to heaven while feeling as though you're on your way to hell.
Sounds wonderful, doesn't it?
May God help you to get right.
Get away.
Get help.
And get busy.

THREE

STRONG MEN TEND TO IGNORE GOOD ADVICE

*My athletes always follow my advice . . . unless it conflicts
with what they want to do.*

—LOU HOLTZ

Fools think they need no advice, but the wise listen to others.
—SOLOMON (PROVERBS 12:15)

WHEN I RUN ACROSS A GOOD PIECE OF ADVICE, I JOT
it down and stick it in a file. Here are a few of the gems I've
collected:

> When you're depressed, listen to country music. The
> people in the songs will always be more messed up than
> you are.

> Don't worry about flunking algebra. In real life there's no
> such thing as algebra.

Always buy your parents nice gifts. After all, you don't want to inherit junk.

If you're having trouble opening a childproof bottle, leave it in a room with a child.

Don't bother naming your cat. He's not going to come when you call him anyway.

If good advice were gold, we'd all be millionaires. It's the only precious thing in this world that there's no shortage of. Whether you're looking for ways to save money on your taxes or wanting to build a deck onto the back of your house, you can be sure that our age of information has produced a specialist, book, TV show, hot line, or Web site you can turn to for help.

GOOD ADVICE IS LIKE MEDICINE: IT'S NO GOOD UNLESS YOU TAKE IT.

But good advice is like medicine: It's no good unless you take it. And that's where a lot of strong men run into trouble. Call it pride. Call it stubbornness. Call it whatever you want. The fact is, strong men are often bound and determined to do things their own way, even at the risk of disaster.

Our boy Samson is a perfect example.

He and his dream girl from Timnah were all wrong for each other. They had absolutely nothing in common, and as far as we know, had never even had a conversation when Samson first told his parents he intended to marry her. It was brainless physical attraction and it scared his parents to death. They could see that their son was veering dangerously off course. He was fraternizing with the enemy. He was about to throw his integrity away, and with it, any chance the nation might have of being delivered from the dreaded Philistines. It's easy to understand why they objected so strenuously. It's easy to understand why they advised him to find a nice Israelite girl to marry. It's *not* easy to understand why Samson blew them off with a testy response: "Get her for me. She is the one I want" (Judg. 14:3).

My guess is that his parents unwittingly spoiled him. Remember, he was their first, and possibly their only child. Consider also that they knew God had called him to do great things. Every time they watched the little guy running and playing with his friends, their hearts must have fluttered with pride and joy. I can just see them doting on him and making sure he had the best of everything. It doesn't mean they were bad people. Indeed, most of us would have probably done the same thing. But it would explain why, by the age of twenty, he had become so cocky and self-absorbed.

But in the end it doesn't matter how he got there. The bottom line is that he stands as an eternal example of what can happen when strong, capable men close their ears to good advice. Samson ultimately married the girl against his parents' wishes and set in motion a chain of events that brought him nothing but frustration and heartache.

If you're a strong man, you need to ask yourself how you measure up in this area. Do you feel embarrassed when you have to ask for advice?

Do you bristle when someone challenges your way of doing things?

Have there been times when you have recklessly disregarded good advice just to prove that nobody can tell you what to do?

Would you be forced to admit that you've done some pretty dumb things purely out of stubbornness?

If so, you're in danger of becoming a victim of the Samson Syndrome. Let me see if I can help you chart a new course by directing your mind toward a couple of important facts.

THE GREATEST MEN COVET
GOOD ADVICE

Does the name Butch Harmon ring a bell? If you're a golf enthusiast, it probably does. Butch Harmon is Tiger Woods's personal coach. Since the age of seventeen, Tiger's been depending on Harmon to monitor every aspect of his game. Sure, Tiger knows as much about golf as Butch Harmon, and he's certainly a more talented golfer. But Tiger understands that success often requires more than knowledge and talent. Sometimes it requires another set of eyes. Essentially, Tiger Woods pays Butch Harmon to see things that he's unable to see. Tiny flaws in his stance, his grip, his swing, or his attitude. Flaws that you and I would never notice, but that could easily cost him a victory in the highly competitive world of professional golf.

This is also why every U.S. President from Washington to Bush has surrounded himself with cabinet officers and advisors. It's not a sign of weakness. It's simply an admission that no matter how intelligent or gifted the man in the Oval Office is, it's impossible for him to see every nuance of every problem and identify every possible solution.

Want a biblical example?

Try Moses.

In the early days of the Exodus, Moses' father-in-law, Jethro, paid him a visit. On the very first day he spotted a huge problem that Moses was apparently oblivious to. The problem was that all of Moses' time was being spent acting as a judge for people who had complaints against each other. Imagine *The People's Court* in bathrobes and sandals and you're starting to get the picture. Cranky, ill-tempered people stood in line from daylight until dark, waiting for the opportunity to have Moses hear and settle their disputes. Jethro immediately saw the problem and offered some very good advice:

> "This is not good!" his father-in-law exclaimed. "You're going to wear yourself out—and the people, too. This job is too heavy a burden for you to handle all by yourself. Now let me give you a word of advice, and may God be with you. You should continue to be the people's representative before God, bringing him their questions to be decided. You should tell them God's decisions, teach them God's laws and instructions, and show them how to conduct their lives. But find some capable, honest men who fear God and hate bribes. Appoint them as judges over groups of one thousand, one hundred, fifty, and ten."
> (Exod. 18:17–21)

To Moses' everlasting credit, he didn't snap at Jethro and tell him to mind his own business. Verse 24 says, "Moses listened to his father-in-law's advice and followed his suggestions."

The point is, even the brightest and best among us occasionally need advice. Sometimes we get so engrossed in our work that we can't see what we're doing wrong. Or maybe we've been thinking and acting a certain way for so long that we've grown numb to the consequences we're suffering. Or maybe our limited experience prevents us from seeing the dangers a certain course of action may hold. That's when we need a friend or counselor to speak up.

The next time someone offers you a piece of advice, be careful how you react. Your first tendency will probably be to bristle up and argue. But before you do, stop and consider that maybe the person is looking at something you can't see.

THE GREATEST MEN CHOOSE
GOOD ADVISORS

Good advice comes only from good advisors, so it's important that you give some thought to whom you're going to listen to. Throughout your lifetime, thousands of people will offer you advice and most of it will be unsolicited. Trying to sift through it all can be a daunting task. The best thing to do is make up your mind ahead of time whom you should and shouldn't be listening to. Let me offer you a list of people you definitely *should* be listening to. That's not to say you should do everything they say, but you should at least consider their suggestions.

First, you should be listening to people who disagree with you. Of course, this is the one thing most of us are tempted not to do. People who disagree with us tend to make us mad, especially if they have an irritating manner. When they try to talk to us, we immediately throw up walls. Or we dig in our heels and stubbornly argue with every word they say.

But think about it.

If the only people you ever listen to are the ones who agree with you, your mind will never be stretched, your actions will never be challenged, and your course will never be altered, even though it might need to be.

It's said that Woodrow Wilson once asked a member of his staff to identify the most intelligent, most informed, and most eloquent member of the opposing political party.

"What for?" the staffer asked.

"Because I want to hire him," Wilson responded.

"Hire him? What in the world for?"

"I want him to keep me from going blind," Wilson said.

Before you willingly blind yourself to all opposing points of view, stop and consider a simple but powerful truth that President Wilson must have understood: The world is full of people who have achieved great success without doing things your way.

Second, you should be listening to people who love you. For some reason, this is another group of people we are often reluctant to listen to. A teenager, for example, will tune out his parents, but if his coach gives him the very same piece of advice, he'll hang on every word. Or a husband may call his wife a nag if she tries to give him some advice, but if his boss says the very same thing, he'll jump all over it.

> THE WORLD IS FULL OF PEOPLE WHO HAVE ACHIEVED GREAT SUCCESS WITHOUT DOING THINGS YOUR WAY.

Part of the problem here is familiarity. It may not breed contempt, but it often does breed discourtesy. I'm sure you've noticed how a husband and wife can be ill-tempered and snippy with each other, but sweet as sugar to everyone else. One husband made the mistake of challenging his wife on this very point. Referring to a man they had just spoken to, he said, "Why are you so nice to him and so mean to me?" His wife shot back, "Because it wasn't his snoring that kept me awake all night!"

Irritations aside, you need to listen to the people who love you. Not just the people who *say* they love you, but the people who have *proven* it over time. They may not always give the best advice, and sometimes they might offer it in a way that grates on your nerves, but chances are good that they'll have your best interest at heart. And for that reason alone, they deserve to be heard.

Third, you should be listening to people who have achieved the success you're longing for. I'll never forget talking to a young man about his shaky marriage several years ago. He and his wife had been married for a few years and the relationship was growing increasingly difficult. As we talked, he said, "I'm really trying. My dad has been giving me some pointers, but nothing seems to be helping."

I snapped to attention, not believing what I'd just heard.

"Excuse me," I said. "Did you say your dad has been giving you pointers?"

"Yes, he's trying to help me out."

"How many times has your dad been married?"

"Four."

I said nothing, letting the truth hang in midair like the Goodyear Blimp. Would he see it? Thankfully, he did.

"Maybe he's not the person I should be listening to," he offered.

"That's possible," I said. (What I *wanted* to say was that getting marriage tips from his dad was like taking lessons on anger management from Bobby Knight.)

My friend, the next time somebody offers you some advice, stop and ask yourself a few basic questions:

Does this person have any expertise in this area?

Has he been where you want to go?

What has happened to others who've listened to his advice?

Would you be happy to follow in his footsteps?

If you can't formulate a positive response to these basic questions, it's very unlikely that the person will have any meaningful advice to offer you.

Fourth, you should be listening to people who demonstrate wisdom. Proverbs 15:7 says, "Only the wise can give good advice." The thing to remember here is that sometimes wisdom comes wrapped in some funny-looking packages. It's not always the alphabet guy—the CEO with the M.A. and Ph.D from UCLA—who has the most wisdom. Sometimes it's the person you'd least expect.

A few years ago the wire services carried a story about a man who worked as a custodian for over fifty years. He was an outgoing fellow who made friends easily and was called "Pop" by everyone who knew him. He had no formal education, wore scruffy old clothes, and never drove a car that was newer than fifteen years old. Yet when he died it was learned that he owned investments worth over two and a half million dollars!

But here's the kicker.

For the last ten years of his life he was the custodian for an investment firm. Imagine! Every night he emptied the wastebaskets of men and women who were supposed to be experts in the stock market, yet every one of them would have given anything to have his portfolio!

Never judge a book by its cover. Sometimes people are sharper than they look.

And finally, you should be listening to people who know and love God's Word. Proverbs 2:6 says, "The LORD grants wisdom! From his mouth come knowledge and understanding." All you have to do to appreciate the wisdom of God is look at what the wisdom of men has given us. The following laws are real and were passed by elected officials who were judged by their constituents to be wise and intelligent:

> In Alabama it is illegal to drive a car while blindfolded.

> In Connecticut it is illegal to walk across a street on your hands.

> In Illinois it is illegal to give a lighted cigar to a dog, cat, or any other domesticated animal.

> In Massachusetts it is illegal to snore with your bedroom windows open.

> In Oklahoma it is illegal to make ugly faces at a dog.

> In Kentucky it is illegal to carry an ice-cream cone in your pocket.

No wonder Proverbs 3:7 says, "Don't be impressed with your own wisdom." Throughout history, men have said and done some incredibly dumb things. Therefore, when you find a person who knows and loves God's Word, someone who has not only studied it, but built his life on its principles and precepts, you need to listen very carefully. Such people often have rare and unique insights to offer, insights that can truly be a light for your path (Ps. 119:105).

Before I close this chapter, I want to say a word about this business of listening. I've been talking about whom you should listen to, but the simple truth is that if you don't know *how* to listen, it doesn't much matter whom you listen to.

NBA legend Bill Russell tells a funny story about his days as a TV analyst. He was doing commentary for ABC during a playoff series between the Lakers and the Knicks. About a week after the series ended, he got a letter from an irate Lakers fan wanting to know why he hated the Lakers. In the same batch of mail he got another letter from an equally irate Knicks fan wanting to know why he hated the Knicks. In a moment of true inspiration, Russell grabbed a couple of envelopes and sent the letter from the Knicks fan to the Lakers fan and the letter from the Lakers fan to the Knicks fan.

> HE KNOWS THAT IF YOU GET MAD AT THE MESSENGER, YOU'LL COMPLETELY MISS ANY WISDOM THAT MAY BE IN THE MESSAGE.

If nothing else, that story illustrates that somewhere between the lips and the ears, crazy things can happen to the spoken word. So let me give you six quick tips on how to listen when somebody offers you advice. These tips will help ensure that what you're hearing is actually what's being said.

First, RESERVE judgment. It's easy to tune someone out before he ever starts talking simply because you know what he's going to say. But even if you think you know what's coming, listen anyway. Sometimes a friend can frame the truth in a way that's fresh and enlightening. He might come up with an angle you haven't thought of. His idea might be the one that makes all the difference.

Second, RESIST the temptation to butt in. You should have learned in kindergarten that interrupting is rude. It also creates confusion by fragmenting thoughts. If you've ever watched the

CNN program *Crossfire*, you know that when people are constantly interrupting each other, the truth suffers.

Third, REMAIN calm, especially if the person you're listening to becomes agitated or uses inflammatory language. Keep in mind that anger is one of Satan's most effective tools. He knows that if you get mad at the messenger, you'll completely miss any wisdom that may be in the message.

Fourth, REVIEW for purposes of clarification. When the person has stated his case and you're still not sure exactly what he means, you can paraphrase what you just heard and ask, "Is that what you're saying?" If it isn't, then keep asking questions until you get it straight.

Fifth, REFLECT on the advice itself. Pray about it and search the Scriptures to determine God's will in the matter. Imagine yourself following the suggested course of action. What might happen? How would your life be changed? How would others be affected?

Sixth, RECEIVE or REJECT. As I said earlier, you do not have to take anyone's advice. Over the course of your life you'll undoubtedly reject a lot more advice than you'll take. My point is simply that you should work through this process to avoid making a hasty, thoughtless decision.

If you're a strong man, you're probably a good talker. I'm guessing that you're never more comfortable than when you're barking orders and watching people scurry to do your bidding. But the noted Englishman, Benjamin Disraeli, once observed that God gave us two ears and one mouth because He intended for us to do twice as much listening as talking. Solomon said, "Tune your ears to wisdom" (Prov. 2:2), and "Plans go wrong for lack of advice" (15:22). And Jesus himself said, "He who has an ear, let him hear . . ." (Rev. 2:7, NASB).

The next time you're tempted to turn a deaf ear to somebody who's offering you a piece of advice, remember these exhortations and stop and think about Samson. When he ignored his parents, it's as if his doom was sealed. From that point on, we see him becoming more and more reckless. We see him drifting farther away from his calling and sinking deeper into sin. Yes, it took years for him to finally hit rock bottom, but it's clear that the downward course of his life was set the moment he closed his ears to a piece of very good advice.

Don't make the same mistake.

STRONG MEN TEND TO BREAK RULES

No rules, just right.

—OUTBACK STEAKHOUSE SLOGAN

Loving God means keeping his commandments.

—JOHN THE APOSTLE (1 JOHN 5:3)

SAMSON'S STORY HAS ALL THE SUBTLETY OF A FOGHORN. From start to finish, it blasts you with one hair-raising escapade after another. From the blood-stained battlefields of Lehi to the silky softness of a beautiful traitor's bed, Samson was almost constantly in danger. Yet he never seemed to mind. In fact, it appears that he was never happier than when he was flirting with disaster.

But there was at least one tranquil moment in Samson's life. A rare moment when there were no enemies lurking in the shadows, when Samson's sexual desire was under control, and when he wasn't plotting or carrying out some sophomoric prank.

Unfortunately, even in that quiet moment, Samson found a way to sin. And the sin he committed tells us as much about him as any of his sexual affairs or battlefield adventures.

Let me give you the background.

Though I'm sure they never felt good about it, Samson's parents eventually acquiesced to his wishes regarding the girl from Timnah and accompanied him to the Philistine village to arrange the wedding. At some point during the journey, Samson left his parents and galloped off into a nearby vineyard, probably to get them all something to eat. But Samson wasn't the only hungry creature prowling the vineyard that day. The Bible says a vicious young lion was also lurking there and was determined to have Samson for lunch.

When I was in high school, I worked afternoons and Saturdays at a furniture store in my hometown of West Salem, Illinois. It was a rural area, and we often had to make deliveries to farmhouses well out in the country. One afternoon my boss and I were carrying a hide-a-bed sofa across a farmer's front yard when, suddenly, a German shepherd came tearing around the corner of the house, barking for all he was worth. I remember hoping that he had his eye on a rabbit or a cat. Anything other than my leg. But there was no rabbit or cat in sight and in seconds the dog was treating my leg like an ear of corn.

We dropped the sofa, and I began a futile attempt to get away. I spun and kicked and shouted, but the dog hung on. Then my boss got into the act, showing the form of an NFL place kicker as he tried to boot the dog in the hindquarters. (Unfortunately, he didn't show the *aim* of an NFL place kicker!) Finally, the owner came running out of the house and down the front steps to pull the dog off of me. I collapsed, breathing as if I'd just run a marathon, and inspected the damage. My jeans were ripped and I had bloody teeth marks on my leg.

My mind always goes back to that incident when I think about Samson being attacked by a lion. There I was, flopping around helplessly, totally at the mercy of that demented dog, while Samson coolly "ripped the lion's jaws apart with his bare hands." I rationalize this obvious disparity in our self-defense techniques by pointing out that Samson had some help. Judges 14:6 says that just before he ripped the lion apart, "the Spirit of the Lord powerfully took control of him."

Now jump ahead a few weeks.

The time for the wedding had arrived and Samson was making one last trip to Timnah to tie the knot. On the way, he remembered his encounter with the lion and wondered what had become of the carcass. Deciding to have a look, he veered off the road and made his way to the scene of the struggle. What he found was the carcass and a swarm of bees that were calling it home. This was unusual because bees aren't normally found in cadavers. Flies and maggots are, but not bees. Yet there they were, along with a nice big wad of mouth-watering honey.

OK, time out.

This is where we need to stop and do some serious thinking. Most people blow right through this part of the story without realizing the significance of it. They assume that because Samson is not fighting the Philistines or playing Twister with a member of the opposite sex, it's not an important passage. But nothing could be farther from the truth. Indeed, this may well be *the* most important scene in Samson's life story because it's the one occasion when he was under no pressure whatsoever—either from enemies or hormones. The sun was shining, birds were chirping, and there wasn't a good-looking woman anywhere around. Yet, he still found a way to sin.

It all had to do with Samson's Nazirite vow. The vow stated that anything unclean was strictly off limits. And since contact with a corpse made any object unclean (Lev. 11:24–25), the honey was a major no-no. And don't think Samson didn't know it. He was raised by godly parents who would have taken great pains to teach him the finer points of the Old-Testament Law. You can be sure Samson knew full well what the rules were.

The thing is, he didn't care.

He dismissed any thoughts of the Law from his mind, shooed the bees away, stuck his fingers into that big glob of honey, and had himself a delicious afternoon snack. No doubt he leaned on the old tree-falling-in-the-forest conundrum: If a tree falls in the forest and no one is there to hear it, did it make a sound? Samson probably thought, *If a man breaks a rule and no one is there to see it, did it happen?*

Here we come face to face with yet another aspect of the Samson Syndrome. Strong men in all walks of life are often inclined to stretch, bend, and even break the rules with little regard for the consequences. Think back over the last fifteen years and quite a few prominent rule breakers will come to mind:

> ALEX RODRIGUEZ (Suspended 211 games for use of a banned substance)
>
> ANTHONY WEINER (Tweeted obscene pictures of himself to a woman who was not his wife)
>
> BRETT FAVRE (Tweeted inappropriate messages to a woman who was not his wife)

PRESIDENT BILL CLINTON (had an affair with a White
House intern)

CORY MONTEITH (Died as a result of heroin use)

GENERAL DAVID PETRAEUS (Lost his career due to an
extra-marital affair)

JESSE JACKSON (fathered a child out of wedlock)

MIKE TYSON (bit off a chunk of his opponent's ear during
competition)

PETER WARRICK (caught working a scam at a Dillard's
department store)

WILLIE NELSON (indicted for tax evasion to the tune of
16 million dollars)

Of course, these are just a few of the high-profile strong men
who got caught breaking rules. There are no doubt many others
who haven't gotten caught, and many more who aren't famous
enough for us to hear about: men
who cheat on their wives, pad
their expense accounts, lie to their
bosses (or their employees), cheat
on their taxes, take bribes, use
drugs, drive too fast, and violate
every rule of good health known
to man.

> STRONG MEN BELIEVE THAT
> THEIR GREAT STRENGTH IS THEIR
> SAFETY NET, THAT NO MATTER
> WHAT HAPPENS, THEY'LL BE ABLE
> TO THINK, TALK, OR MUSCLE
> THEIR WAY OUT OF TROUBLE.

While it's true that people in all walks of life are rule breakers,
you will often find a brazenness in strong men that is shocking.
For example, when it was revealed that Bill Clinton was engaging
in sex acts with an intern in or near the Oval Office, America was
stunned. His actions were a vivid illustration that great strength
brings with it a feeling of invincibility. As I pointed out in chapter

1, strong men believe that their great strength is their safety net, that no matter what happens, they'll be able to think, talk, or muscle their way out of trouble.

If you are a rule breaker, and especially if your rule breaking has become increasingly brazen and reckless, you need to stop and reflect on the value of rules. There are three ways rules help us.

RULES SHELTER US FROM TROUBLE

Robert Downey Jr. is an extraordinary actor who was nominated for an Academy Award in 1992. At thirty-six, he should be at the peak of his career, racking up awards and making millions of dollars a year. Instead, he's a rule breaker, a drug addict who's piled up enough legal problems to keep him under court supervision for years to come. He's lost jobs and marriages, done jail time, been confined to treatment facilities, endured physical pain, and suffered extreme emotional anguish. You've seen him on the news being ushered into courtroom after courtroom looking tired and disheveled. In a national television interview he spoke of his misery and even questioned whether life was worth living. Robert Downey Jr. is a tragic example of how troubles mount for people who continually break rules.

But what about one time rule breakers? What about guys who just get a little carried away and do something crazy on a whim? Do they also suffer?

Ask David Wesley, of the Charlotte Hornets.

He and teammate Bobby Phills were leaving practice on January 12, 2000. In a classic boys-will-be-boys scenario, they jumped into their Porsches and sped away from the Charlotte

Coliseum. Eyewitnesses said they were racing at speeds in excess of seventy-five miles an hour in a forty-five mile-an-hour zone. Suddenly, Phills, whose personalized license plate read SLAMN, lost control of his car and crashed head-on into a minivan. He was killed instantly and had to be cut out of the car. Law-enforcement officers reported that the skid marks from his vehicle were several hundred feet long. Tragically, Phills, who was only thirty, left behind his wife, Kendall, and two young children. David Wesley was not involved in the accident.

Or was he?

In the end, Wesley was convicted of reckless driving, but whatever penalty he was forced to pay will surely pale in comparison with the ache in his heart. The whole thing was undoubtedly just a testosterone flare-up. A couple of macho guys fooling around, playing fast and loose with the rules. No one was supposed to get hurt.

No one ever is.

Right now you could probably name a dozen rules that you feel are a hindrance to your happiness. Some may be man-made and others may be biblical. Some may be merely annoying and others may seem to be ruining your life by robbing you of your greatest hopes and dreams. No doubt you've tried to find ways around them. Maybe you've even tested the waters by breaking one or two.

Rest assured. Everybody feels this way at one time or another.

However, it's a feeling you need to fight with every ounce of your being, for the Scriptures continually hammer away at the importance of obedience.

Psalm 119:2: "Happy are those who obey his decrees and search for him with all their hearts."

> *Romans 13:1–2:* "Obey the government, for God is the one who put it there. All governments have been placed in power by God. So those who refuse to obey the laws of the land are refusing to obey God, and punishment will follow."

> *Ephesians 6:1:* "Children, obey your parents because you belong to the Lord, for this is the right thing to do."

> *Ephesians 6:5:* "Slaves, obey your earthly masters with deep respect and fear. Serve them sincerely as you would serve Christ."

Notice these verses say nothing about us *liking* the rules and laws that are imposed upon us. In fact, the clear implication of these verses is that we *won't* always like the rules that are imposed on us by God, the government, our parents, or our employers. But obey them we must, if we want to stay out of trouble.

RULES SHAPE US INTO BETTER PEOPLE

Children are extremely impressionable. That's why, if you're a conscientious parent, you have established a number of rules for your children to abide by. No doubt you monitor what they watch and listen to, where they go, whom they go with, what time they get home, and so on. The point is not to spoil their fun, but to mold and shape them into decent human beings.

The military does the same thing with its raw recruits. A few years ago a teenage boy from our congregation joined the Marines. When he returned for a visit after basic training, it was as if someone else had taken on his identity. He looked trim and sharp, spoke with dignity, demonstrated excellent manners, and possessed tremendous self-confidence. When I spoke to him about his experience, he said, "They almost killed me." In other words, they imposed strict rules and hard-nosed discipline on him that he'd never had to face before, all for the purpose of turning him into a Marine.

But the greatest example of this is seen in what God did in the Old Testament with His children, the Israelites. He didn't want them to be like the pagan nations that surrounded them, so He used the Ten Commandments and a variety of other rules and regulations to set them on a different course. The Israelites were considered strange, not only for what they did (circumcision), but for what they didn't do (worship idols). Yet every law, from the many dietary restrictions to the detailed sacrificial system, was designed to lead them in the direction of righteousness and to prepare them for the coming Savior (Gal. 3:24).

> THE CLEAR IMPLICATION OF THESE VERSES IS THAT WE WON'T ALWAYS LIKE THE RULES THAT ARE IMPOSED ON US BY GOD, THE GOVERNMENT, OUR PARENTS, OR OUR EMPLOYERS.

All of life is a molding and shaping process. From the time we're born until we die, we are learning, growing, and adapting. Thank God for those people who stepped up at critical moments and used the chisel of a well-chosen rule to chip away your rough edges. Maybe there's a specific person—a coach, teacher, parent, or guardian—that you thought was too tough on you at the time. But now you realize how much that individual helped you. Maybe it's time for you to go back and thank that rule maker for shaping you into a better person.

RULES SHOW US HOW WE'RE DOING

Years ago I was teaching on the Ten Commandments and a young man in the audience seemed particularly interested. I didn't know him very well since he was a newcomer to our church, but I sensed that with each lesson he was being exposed to some ideas he'd never considered before. After the final lesson he approached me, thanked me for the lessons, and then made this stunning comment: "By my count, I have broken nine of the Ten Commandments within the last year. The only thing I haven't done is kill somebody. I guess I've got some work to do."

Indeed he did.

But here's the key. Because God was so gracious in giving us a clear and comprehensive set of rules to govern both our private and public lives, that young man had a place to start, goals to shoot for, and a way of measuring his progress.

So do you.

For your personal life, you have the same Word of God.

For your professional life, you have your job description.

For your finances, you have a budget.

For your health, you have your doctor's orders.

Yes, at times it seems as though we're swamped with rules. But imagine how confusing life would be without them! The only way you can know how you're doing in any area of life is to consult the appropriate rule book.

Before I close this chapter I want to address a question that I know is on your mind. You're thinking, "But aren't there some rules that *should* be broken?"

The answer is, absolutely.

In fact, this truth is one of the central messages of the book of Daniel. When we see Shadrach, Meshach, and Abednego refusing to bow down and worship a gold statue in spite of King Nebuchadnezzar's decree (Dan. 3:16–18), and then we see Daniel continuing to worship his God in spite of Darius's prohibitions (Dan. 6:13), and then we see all of them being miraculously protected by God when the hammer came down, there can be no doubt that God approves of the breaking of some rules.

The trick is to know which ones.

Let me suggest five common-sense questions you can ask that should help you accurately evaluate any rule.

Question #1: Who wrote the rule? Obviously, if God wrote it, you should follow it. However, if a man wrote it, then you would do well to consider the man. Does he have the authority to be writing rules? Does he have credibility or expertise in the area where he's exerting control? Does he have common sense? What are his motivations?

Question #2: Does the rule ask you to do anything that would violate God's will or your conscience? Last fall during the baseball playoffs, the Fox announcers had to read a promo for a cable program called *The Best Damn Sports Show, Period.* As I watched, I noticed that one announcer in particular always substituted the word *darn* for *damn.* He didn't make a show of it and offered no editorial comment. He simply made the substitution and went right on. I don't know the announcer. I have no idea if he's a Christian. But it's pretty obvious that the word *damn* violated his conscience. I give him a lot of credit for having the courage to bend the rule.

Question #3: Does the rule have a meaningful purpose? Be careful with this question. If you don't like the rule's purpose, you will be tempted to say it's not meaningful. However, sometimes it's the most distasteful rules that are the best for us.

One high-school basketball coach got sick and tired of his players missing crucial free throws, so he instituted a rule that the players had to run ten extra laps around the gym for every free throw they missed in a game. Naturally, the players protested. Some of them piled up so many laps that they had to stay after practice and run for an extra half hour. They complained that the rule was breaking their spirit and harming team morale. But guess what.

> TAKE ANY RULE YOU CAN THINK OF AND ASK YOURSELF WHAT WOULD HAPPEN IF EVERYBODY DISOBEYED IT. YOUR IMAGINATION WILL TELL YOU IF IT'S A GOOD RULE.

The team's free-throw percentage began to climb. It went from 58 percent to 69 percent. But the biggest result was that the team began to win more games, including a one point nail-biter against a tough conference opponent on—you guessed it—a last-second free throw.

Question #4: What would happen if you disobeyed the rule? Would you get fired? Would you get arrested? Would you ruin your marriage? I never cease to be amazed at the number of seemingly intelligent people who break both the rules of law and common sense, knowing full well that doing so will bring them deep trouble.

Question #5: What would happen if everybody disobeyed the rule? If you're familiar with the Orlando area, you know that the intersection of I-4 and State Road 535 is one of the busiest interchanges in the world. It's one of the main jumping-off points for Disneyworld, and it's almost always a zoo. Recently there was a power failure in that area right at the peak of rush hour. Not a single traffic light was working, and yours truly happened to be right in the middle of it. Never in my life have I seen so much confusion—and so many short tempers! But as I worked my way through the pandemonium, it occurred to me that this is what it would be like if *everybody* ignored all the rules of the road.

Take any rule you can think of and ask yourself what would happen if everybody disobeyed it. Your imagination will tell you if it's a good rule.

The truth is, most rules are good and should be obeyed. As a strong man, you might be tempted to pull a Samson and ignore the ones that cramp your style. But rest assured, it will catch up with you sooner or later, just as it did with Samson. Habitual rule breakers always end badly.

FIVE

STRONG MEN TEND TO OVERESTIMATE THEIR OWN CLEVERNESS

Only two things are infinite: the universe and human stupidity. And I'm not sure about the universe.

—ALBERT EINSTEIN

People ruin their lives by their own foolishness.

—SOLOMON (PROVERBS 19:3)

THERE IS SOMETHING STRANGELY SATISFYING ABOUT the misadventures of hapless criminals. One young man in particular comes to mind as I begin this chapter.

He noticed that every Friday at 10:00 A.M. an armored car would pull up in front of the bowling alley that was directly across the street from his house. The uniformed guard would go inside and come out a couple of minutes later carrying two or three big bags of money. Probably the entire week's receipts. The young man felt sure that he could jump out of the bushes, hold up the driver, and disappear into the thick woods behind the bowling alley in fifteen seconds or less. Then he would double back to his vehicle, drive around the block, and simply pull into his garage and lower the door. By the time the cops arrived, he would be sitting in his living room with his feet up, drinking a cold beer and watching the action through his picture window like an old episode of *Starsky and Hutch*. Never in a million years would they think of looking for the perpetrator right across the street.

When the day finally came to pull the job, the young man dressed in black and pulled a ski mask over his face. Carrying a shotgun, he crept quietly through the woods behind the bowling alley and took up his position just around the corner from the front entrance. Squatting behind a bush, he watched the armored car pull up and park, right on time. The guard jumped out of the vehicle and walked inside the building. The young man knew from his weeks of observation that in less than three minutes the guard would be coming out, money bags in hand.

He closed his eyes and took a deep breath.

This was it.

The moment of truth.

All of his hard work was about to pay off, big-time.

Suddenly, the door opened and the guard reappeared. The young man jumped from behind the bush and ran toward him. "Give me the bags!" he screamed.

The guard spun around, wide-eyed, dropped the bags, and threw his hands into the air.

The young man grabbed the biggest one. Somehow it seemed heavier and bulkier than he'd anticipated, so he left the others behind and took off for the woods. *There must be a million dollars in here,* he thought, as he scampered through the underbrush.

Meanwhile, the driver walked back into the bowling alley and straight to the proprietor's office.

"You're not going to believe what just happened," he said.

"What?" the proprietor asked.

"A guy with a gun and a ski mask just robbed me."

"He took your wallet?"

"No, just a bag of dirty towels."

You see, what the young man thought was an armored car was actually a laundry truck.

Have you ever done something you thought was really clever, only to realize after the fact that it was really dumb? If so, then you have something in common with that bumbling bandit . . . and with Samson. No one would ever question Samson's intelligence. He was obviously a bright guy. But there were times when he greatly overestimated his cleverness.

Take, for example, the party he threw to celebrate his marriage to the girl from Timnah. Judges 14:10–11 tells us that it was done according to the custom of the day and that thirty young men from the town were invited. It was, to put it bluntly, a great big stag party. A seven-day drinking binge.

Not smart for a guy who's supposed to be living under the Nazirite vow.

At some point during the festivities (possibly while Samson was a bit tipsy) he decided to have a little fun with his Philistine groomsmen. "Let me tell you a riddle," he said. "If you solve my riddle during these seven days of the celebration, I will give you thirty plain linen robes and thirty fancy robes. But if you can't solve it, then you must give me thirty linen robes and thirty fancy robes" (14:12–13).

It's easy to see why the Philistines were eager to take this bet. First, there were thirty of them to put their heads together and they had a full seven days to come up with the answer. Second, the risk was minimal. Even if they failed, it would only cost them one suit of clothes apiece. (The linen robes and the fancy robes were a man's inner and outer garments respectively, making up one complete suit of clothes.) And third, it gave them an opportunity to embarrass the cocky Samson.

To Samson's credit, the riddle was quite clever:

> From the one who eats came something to eat;
> Out of the strong came something sweet. (14:14)

As readers of the narrative, we know this is a reference to the lion he killed in the vineyards outside Timnah (14:5–6) and to the honey he extracted from the lion's carcass a few days later (14:8–9). But the Philistines had no clue what he was referring to, and since there had been no witnesses to the incident, Samson figured there was no way they could ever find out. Thus, he believed he was guaranteed to win the bet.

Very clever. Except for one thing. Samson didn't count on the Philistines cheating to get the answer.

When they realized they were hopelessly stumped and in danger of looking like fools, they resorted to treachery. They approached Samson's new wife in secret and threatened to burn her father's house down with her in it if she didn't discover the answer to the riddle and reveal it to them before the deadline passed. Naturally, Samson's wife pulled out all the stops in an effort to learn the answer. (Who wouldn't?) She begged, whined, and cried until Samson couldn't stand it anymore. Finally, on the seventh day, with his nerves completely shot from his new wife's constant nagging, he gave in and told her the answer. Apparently, she had just enough time to pass it on to the groomsmen, who announced it just before sundown on the seventh day, thus winning the bet and making the clever Samson look like a complete fool.

> DISCERNMENT . . . THE SIMPLE KNACK OF KNOWING WHERE AND WHEN TO DRAW THE LINE.

Samson's fatal mistake in this situation was that he misjudged his Philistine groomsmen. He assumed they would play by the rules. There was no reason why he *should* have assumed that. There was nothing in their character to indicate the slightest trace of integrity. They were Samson's rivals in every sense of the term and wanted nothing more than to embarrass him. He should have known they would cheat. But apparently he didn't think about it.

In a word, what Samson lacked was discernment. John Maxwell defines discernment as the ability to see through to the heart of a matter.

It's wisdom.

Good judgment.

The simple knack of knowing where and when to draw the line.

The reason why strong men tend to fall prey to this aspect of the Samson Syndrome is because they are especially susceptible to discernment's seven deadliest enemies, all of which are mentioned in the book of Proverbs.

THE ENEMIES OF DISCERNMENT

First, there is PRIDE. Proverbs 16:18 is a verse that every strong man should memorize. It says, "Pride goes before destruction, and haughtiness before a fall."

In the riddle affair we get a crystal-clear snapshot of Samson's pride. He obviously wanted to embarrass his Philistine grooms-men. You just know he was going to gloat when they surren-dered at the end of seven days and handed over their thirty suits of clothes. It's as if he was sensitive to his "new kid on the block" status and wanted to prove that he was a man to be reckoned with.

The problem is that Samson's pride caused him to *overesti-mate* his own ability and *underestimate* his opponent's, which is what always happens. Think about Japan during World War II. It seems unfathomable now, but the Japanese actually thought they could take on the United States and win. They were proud of their military might and saw their plan to hit Pearl Harbor with a surprise attack as a stroke of genius. But it was a horrible miscalculation, as they realized a few years later when two of their greatest cities lay in ruins and three hundred thousand Japanese civilians lay dead.

The second deadly enemy of discernment is LIQUOR. It shouldn't come as a surprise to anybody that Samson's foolish contest was initiated during a drunken bash. Booze and clear thinking have never gone together, as Solomon suggested when he said, "Who-ever is led astray by drink cannot be wise" (Proverbs 20:1).

Recently, there was a story in the news about a college football player who thought it would be clever to climb out his dorm room window, inch his way along a narrow ledge, and burst into the room next door where some coeds were having a party. Tragically, he fell three stories and broke his back and leg. It was determined that the alcohol content in his blood was twice the legal limit.

Stories like that are in the news every day. I asked a police officer not long ago if he could estimate the percentage of crimes and mishaps he responds to that are alcohol related. He scratched his chin and said, "Probably 75 percent or more."

The third deadly enemy of discernment is ANGER. We learned just how deadly this one can be during the highly publicized trial of Thomas Junta. On July 5, 2000, he attended his son's hockey practice and felt that the coach, Michael Costin, allowed the boys to play a little too rough. After practice, Junta confronted Costin, angry words were exchanged, and a fight broke out. According to eyewitnesses, Junta, who outweighed Costin by over a hundred pounds, completely overpowered the smaller man and beat him senseless. Michael Costin died two days later as a result of the blows, which ruptured an artery in his brain. Junta was convicted of involuntary manslaughter and will spend six to ten years in prison.

Proverbs 27:4 says, "Anger is cruel, and wrath is like a flood."

The fourth deadly enemy of discernment is LUST. We've already examined the problem of lust, but here it must be mentioned again, for few things will cloud a man's judgment more completely. Proverbs 6:32 says, "The man who commits adultery is an utter fool, for he destroys his own soul."

Not to mention his marriage.

Several years ago, a major airline launched a promotional campaign called "Fly Your Wife for Free." It was an encouragement for businessmen to take their wives with them on out-of-town trips. Any man who chose to take advantage of the promotion was sent a letter of thanks along with an encouragement to fly again soon.

Can you guess what happened?

The airline had to cancel the program because they started getting hundreds of phone calls from angry wives who had just opened the letters. They knew *they* hadn't been on any business trips with their husbands, so they were demanding to know who their husbands *had* taken with them!

Imagine hundreds of powerful executives, jet-setting around the country with their secret lovers, thinking they are so very clever. Then one day they walk into the house and find that they've been busted!

The fifth deadly enemy of discernment is GREED. Proverbs 1:18–19 is a passage for our generation if there ever was one. It says, "They set an ambush for themselves; they booby-trap their own lives! Such is the fate of all who are greedy for gain. It ends up robbing them of life."

A. Alfred Taubman could tell us all about it.

Taubman was the chairman of Sotheby's auction house, a fabulously wealthy and highly respected man who lived with his wife, Judy, at the very top of international society. He literally had all the money he would ever be able to spend. But greed is never content, so Mr. Taubman illegally conspired with Sir Anthony Tennant of Christie's auction house to fix prices so that the sellers of fine art and jewelry couldn't play one house against the other. It seemed like such a clever idea. That is, until Mr. Taubman heard the crack of a gavel in federal court, followed by the jury foreman's pronouncement: "Guilty!"

The sixth deadly enemy of discernment is HATRED. When you harbor resentment toward someone and long to get revenge, you tend to lose all perspective. Police records are loaded with stories of people who have done clever but foolhardy things in an effort to even a score.

Consider a tragic case from southern California. A college student was furious with his girlfriend for dumping him, so he decided to pay her back. Knowing she was terrified of snakes, he thought it would be clever to catch a snake and turn it loose in her apartment. He and a couple of his fraternity brothers managed to round up a harmless, garden-variety snake and released it through her doggy door while she was at work. The next morning, the girl pulled back the shower curtain and saw the snake stretched out across the tile floor. The fright caused her to stumble backwards. She fell, hit her head against the vanity, fractured her skull, and died. The students, who had told several friends about their "clever" prank, were taken into custody.

Proverbs 26:26 says, "While their hatred may be concealed by trickery, it will finally come to light for all to see."

The seventh deadly enemy of discernment is IMPATIENCE. This one may look like the most innocent of the seven, but it could in fact be the most costly in terms of damage and dollars. Consider the problem of speeding, for example. Impatient people get behind the wheel of a car and seem to lose all sense of reason. They stomp down on the accelerator, dart in and out of traffic, run red lights, cut off other drivers, and in the process create a public health hazard that is second to none. According to the National Highway Traffic Safety Administration, the economic cost of speeding to our society is almost thirty billion dollars a year. It is a contributing factor in 30 percent of all fatal crashes. About fifteen thousand lives a year are lost in speeding-related accidents.

Proverbs 27:12 says, "A prudent person foresees the danger ahead and takes precautions." In other words, he slows down and moves ahead carefully and thoughtfully.

If you have a weakness in just one of these seven areas, it could be enough to have you making some very foolish decisions. But if, like Samson, you're weak in several of them, your life is probably a complete mess even as you're reading these words.

So let me share with you the four secrets of discernment that will help you start making some better decisions.

THE SECRETS OF DISCERNMENT

We can see them clearly in the life of Joseph, one of the strongest men in the Old Testament. In Genesis 39, we find him in Egypt, serving as the manager of Potiphar's household. Potiphar was the captain of the palace guard and a member of Pharaoh's cabinet. He'd recognized Joseph's organizational and leadership skills and decided to entrust everything he owned to Joseph's care. The problem was that Potiphar's wife was equally impressed with Joseph, only for a different reason. She found him to be incredibly sexy and was determined to get him into her bed. She was probably a good-looking woman, and was certainly a woman of privilege, who was used to getting whatever she wanted. Joseph probably wasn't the first employee she tried to seduce. However, he may well have been the first to turn her down.

Joseph's handling of Potiphar's wife's shameful behavior is a study in discernment. He properly assessed the situation and handled everything from her mildly flirtatious comments to her final brazen overture with perfect judgment. A close look at Genesis 39:7–12 will reveal how he did it.

First, he LOOKED AROUND and saw his blessings. In verse 8, Joseph said to Potiphar's wife, "Look, my master trusts me with everything in his entire household. No one here has more authority than I do." That was really saying something when you stop to consider that Joseph had been sold into slavery as a boy and spent two years in prison as a young man. He, better than anyone, realized how blessed he was to be in such a privileged position. The last thing he wanted to do was jeopardize it all by sleeping with his boss's wife.

> LOOK AT YOUR WIFE, YOUR CHILDREN, YOUR HOME, YOUR JOB, AND ALL THE OTHER GOOD THINGS THAT HAVE COME INTO YOUR LIFE. THEN ASK YOURSELF IF A FEW MINUTES' WORTH OF PLEASURE IS WORTH JEOPARDIZING ALL THAT.

The next time you're faced with an opportunity to do something a little wild and crazy, you need to stop and look around. Look at your wife, your children, your home, your job, and all the other good things that have come into your life. Then ask yourself if a few minutes' worth of pleasure is worth jeopardizing all that.

Second, Joseph LOOKED WITHIN and saw his integrity. Sometimes it's not what you have, but what you *are* that weighs heaviest in the decision-making process. Joseph said, "How could I ever do such a wicked thing?" (39:9) No doubt there were some on the household staff that would have given anything to sleep with Potiphar's wife (and a few probably already had!). But Joseph wasn't one of them. He'd chosen to live by a higher moral code. Thus, he knew that even if no one ever found out about their tryst, he would have to live with the shame of it himself.

Right now there are a lot of men who've been successful at hiding their sins. They've been very clever and they've managed to avoid detection. Maybe you're one of them. Maybe you've perfected a foolproof system that enables you to indulge in sin without your wife or kids or coworkers even suspecting anything's going on. If so, I'm guessing that you don't feel real good about yourself. A friend of mine used to say, "If you act like a creep, you'll always feel creepy." Joseph obviously understood this and refused to relinquish his self-respect.

Third, Joseph LOOKED FORWARD and saw his future. I love that phrase in verse 9 where Joseph said, "He has held nothing back from me except you, *because you are his wife"* (author's emphasis)! Joseph knew that he had no future with another man's wife. Even if their affair provided a few exotic thrills, it was destined to go down in flames and do more damage than it was worth.

There's been a lot of talk in recent months about airline safety. Would you get on a plane if you knew it stood a 50-percent chance of crashing? How about a 25-percent chance? Still too high? How about a 10-percent chance?

The crazy thing is, lots of strong men get into sinful situations that have a *100-percent* chance of crashing, and never give it a second thought. Then, when the crash happens and their whole world is going up in flames, they wonder why they did it. Believe me, friend. The time to look ahead and anticipate the future is *before* the plane takes off!

Fourth, Joseph LOOKED UP and saw his God. The last line of verse 9 is the clincher. Joseph said, "How could I ever do such a wicked thing? It would be a great sin against God."

Several years ago I counseled a man who had a long history of extramarital affairs. He'd trashed two marriages, but still hadn't learned his lesson. Even as I was meeting with him, he was seeing two or three different women. At one point during our discussions, he made an interesting comment. He said, "I can't help it. A woman's body is the most beautiful thing I've ever seen."

I said, "If you believe that, then I know you've never really taken a good look at God."

At the end of that session, we parted company for good. We ended the counseling process and pretty much went our separate ways. I sensed no change in him at all, and felt very defeated and discouraged. Over the years, I've enjoyed a few victories as a counselor, but just as many failures, and I would have put him at the top of the latter list.

But then a couple of years later, we met again. The moment I saw him I could tell he had changed. His countenance had brightened and his demeanor was more dignified. He seemed happy to see me and anxious to tell me that he'd finally gotten his act together. He told me about his new wife, the church he was attending, and all of the good things that were happening in his life.

I couldn't help it. I simply had to ask, "What happened?"

And the answer he gave put a tear in my eye.

He said, "I finally took a good look at God. And you were right. He *is* the most beautiful thing I've ever seen."

I think that's exactly how Joseph felt. When he looked at God, he simply couldn't bear the thought of sinning.

There's no telling how much different Samson's life would have been if he had consistently employed Joseph's secrets of discernment. If, before ever choosing a course of action, he had looked around, looked within, looked ahead, and looked up, he would have made much better choices and achieved much greater results. With all the blessings and talents God had heaped upon him, he might have been even greater than Moses.

Of course, for him, it's too late.

But it's not for you.

If you're tired of getting burned by your hair-brained schemes and not-so-clever ideas, why don't you try Joseph's secrets? You don't have to sacrifice your fun-loving nature. You can still live with a spirit of adventure. Just try to be more thoughtful. Make sure you're seeing through to the heart of the matter before you go charging full steam ahead.

SIX

STRONG MEN TEND TO USE ANGER AS A TOOL

*Speak when you are angry and you will make the best speech
you will ever regret.*

—AMBROSE BIERCE

Your anger can never make things right in God's sight.
—JAMES, THE HALF-BROTHER OF
JESUS (JAMES 1:20)

WHEN SAMSON REALIZED THAT HIS PHILISTINE
groomsmen had blackmailed his new wife in order to solve his
riddle, he was furious. Judges 14:18–19 gives us a chilling picture
of his rage:

> Samson replied, "If you hadn't plowed with my heifer, you
> wouldn't have found the answer to my riddle!" Then the
> Spirit of the LORD powerfully took control of him. He went
> down to the town of Ashkelon, killed thirty men, took
> their belongings, and gave their clothing to the men who

had answered his riddle. But Samson was furious about what had happened, and he went back home to live with his father and mother.

Samson's anger has been the subject of much debate. In this situation, as well as others, we are told that God's Spirit empowered him when he was blinded by rage. But don't be misled. There's no evidence that his anger had a righteous dimension to it. We don't hear him crying out to God, and there's certainly no evidence that he has repented of any sin. It appears that he was only mad because he'd been made a fool of. He'd been embarrassed and humiliated after acting so cocky. You can be sure that, during this murderous rampage, he wasn't thinking about glorifying God or liberating his people from Philistine bondage; he was simply satisfying his lust for revenge.

Throughout history countless strong men have employed a similar "scorched earth" policy with regard to their personal and business relationships. They simply chew up and spit out anyone who dares to cross them. And there are at least four reasons why they do it, all of which can be seen in a rather embarrassing story from my adolescence.

As a high-school freshman in PE, I was assigned a locker right next to one of the biggest hooligans in the senior class. One day, while I was in the shower, the joker stole my briefs. And not only did he steal them, but he hung them on an overhead light fixture in the middle of the room. When I returned to my locker and realized they were missing, several guys started snickering. One pointed up, and sure enough, there they were in all their glory, hanging just out of my reach.

I turned to Mr. Senior, who was notorious for this sort of

behavior, and demanded that he get them down. Naturally, he declined. So I was faced with a decision. Should I humiliate myself by climbing up on a chair stark naked? (Who knows what they would have done while I was in that compromising position!) Or should I make a stand and fight for my honor . . . not to mention my underwear?

With my anger boiling, I decided to make a stand.

I walked toward Mr. Senior and said, in an even voice, "Get them down."

"No way, José."

And with that, I surprised him. I shoved him with both hands right in the chest and sent him sprawling over a bench and crashing into some lockers. At that moment, the coach stepped around the corner and demanded to know what was going on.

"Atteberry!" he bellowed. "What do you think you're doing?"

"I'm trying to get my underwear back, coach," I said, and pointed to the light fixture above his head.

The coach looked up and did a double take. I could tell he was fighting the urge to smile. Or laugh. Looking back, I don't know how he kept from it. But he did. With a deadpan expression, he looked at Mr. Senior, who was just scrambling to his feet. "Did you put Atteberry's underpants up there?"

"Yes, sir."

"Then get them down. If we're gonna decorate this place, we'll do it with crepe paper and balloons."

And then he turned and walked away.

I'm not proud of myself for resorting to violent behavior in that situation. I certainly wasn't asking, "What would Jesus do?" But I can't deny that four positive things happened as a result:

I got what I wanted (my underwear back).

I created an image of toughness.

I sent a message to other would-be practical jokers.

And I felt a surge of adrenaline-induced euphoria.

Look at those results again. They are the primary reasons why many strong men employ angry outbursts as a matter of routine in both their personal and professional lives. To put it bluntly, explosions of anger get results. They send people scrambling to do your bidding and make you feel like Superman.

Let me ask you five questions. I want you to read them slowly and be brutally honest with your answers.

Question #1: How often do you blow your top? I'm not asking how often you *feel* like blowing it, but how often you actually do it. Once a month? Once a week? Once a day? Once an hour? Does it happen more often than it used to?

Question #2: Do you ever use anger to try to control people? For example, if your wife is pressuring you to do something, do you flare up in anger to make her back off? Do you try to scare your children into behaving? Do you try to intimidate your employees into being more productive?

Question #3: Does it give you satisfaction to know that there are people who are afraid of you? Do you like knowing that people bow to your whims and cater to your desires just so they won't have to face your wrath? Do you love watching your underlings scramble every time you throw a fit?

Question #4: Are your immediate family members afraid of you? Do your wife and children feel comfortable sharing their innermost thoughts with you? Do your kids talk to you about their personal struggles or bypass you and go straight to their mother?

Question #5: Do your angry outbursts ever turn physical? Have you ever thrown something, punched something, or destroyed something in a fit of rage?

Your answers to these questions should tell you if you've fallen prey to this aspect of the Samson Syndrome. If you have, there are two things you need to do.

ANALYZE YOUR ANGER

You may see anger as one of the secrets of your success. You may be able to point to a long list of victories you've won through sheer intimidation. You may be convinced that anger is the one thing you can always count on to turn the tide in your favor.

But wait a minute.

Have you ever really taken a good look at it? Have you ever put your anger under a microscope to see what it's made of? Let me point out four facts concerning anger that you may never have thought about.

First, anger is addictive. It's just like a drug in that it gives you an adrenaline rush and a feeling of invincibility. When you see people leaping into action and scurrying frantically in response to your explosion—or when you see people cowering in fear and bowing to your whims—you can't help but feel like a big, tough guy. It's a great feeling you get every time you blow up. So, just like the addict who keeps sniffing cocaine, you keep blowing up. Pretty soon, anger becomes your identity.

Take Bobby Knight, for example. He is one of the greatest basketball coaches who has ever lived. But I daresay that when you hear his name, the first thing you think about is not a sticky man-to-man defense or a fluid motion offense. Instead, you probably picture flying chairs, profanity-laced tirades, and strangleholds.

Bobby Knight has used anger as a tool for so long—and has done it with so much worldly success—that it has truly become his identity. At this point nobody even *expects* him to stay cool, calm, and collected!

Are you an anger addict?

Have you earned a reputation as a hothead?

Do the people you live and work with walk on eggshells around you for fear of sending you off on a tirade?

Be careful how you answer! Your first impulse will be to laugh these questions off. But remember, that's what Bobby Knight does. He scoffs at the notion that he has a problem with anger, just like an alcoholic claims that he can quit drinking anytime he wants. It's the nature of an addict to live in denial.

Second, anger must be intensified to maintain its effectiveness. I love *The Honeymooners,* the old fifties television series that featured Jackie Gleason as the overbearing Ralph Kramden. You've seen how Ralph rants and raves like a maniac while his wife, Alice, simply sits and waits for the storm to pass. He shakes his fist in her face and tells her that she's going to the moon, but still she doesn't cower in fear.

Why?

Because it's television and it's scripted.

If it were real life, something entirely different would happen, as I learned many years ago when I was first starting out in the ministry.

There was an attractive young woman in our church who often wore long sleeves and high collars, even when the temperature outside was pushing a hundred degrees. One day, at a committee meeting of some sort, I made a lame joke about her being extremely cold natured. She, along with everyone else in the room, let the joke pass without so much as a smile. After the meeting adjourned, another lady on the committee followed me into my office and shut the door.

"Mark, don't you know why she wears long sleeves all the time?"

I had no clue and said so.

"She's hiding bruises."

I was stunned. "What?"

"Her husband abuses her, and she wears those long sleeves and turtlenecks to hide the evidence."

I felt sick to my stomach. I knew her husband was hotheaded by nature, but I never pictured him as a wife beater.

A few weeks later, I seized an opportunity to talk to the woman about the problem, and the story she told was frightening. She said her husband had always had a hot temper and used it to intimidate coworkers and competitors in business. Then he began using the same tactics at home. At first it was just a lot of yelling and screaming. And then one day he hauled off and knocked her across the room.

> ANGER, WHEN USED AS A TOOL, MUST BE INTENSIFIED IN ORDER TO KEEP ACHIEVING THE DESIRED RESULT.

You see, anger, when used as a tool, must be intensified in order to keep achieving the desired result. Hollering and screaming will work for a while, but eventually people will get used to it and tune it out. That's usually when something gets thrown, like a book or a dish. Then something gets punched. Then some*one* gets punched. Then bullets start to fly. Every night on the evening news we hear tragic stories about people who've reached the point of bullets.

You may be a long way from that kind of violence, but you

need to check yourself and see if your anger antics are escalating. Does it frustrate you when people don't respond to your rantings? Do you find that you're having to resort to more outlandish behavior just to get their attention? Have you ever thrown something? Or punched something? If so, what do you think will happen next?

Third, anger produces collateral damage. During our war on terror in Afghanistan, we saw the effectiveness of some incredibly sophisticated weapons. It never ceases to amaze me that we can launch a missile from many miles away and stick it right through our enemy's office window. Yet we still hear reports of collateral damage. Innocent civilians standing nearby may be wounded or killed. Or, in some cases, the wrong building may be targeted. There's simply no getting around the fact that anytime an explosion happens, you run the risk of doing more damage than you intended.

The same is true with explosions of anger.

Not long ago I was in a department store and witnessed a confrontation that ended with a husband calling his wife an ugly name and storming off. The heartbreaking thing was that their little boy, who appeared to be about four, heard every word. My guess is that someday, twenty or so years from now, he'll be talking to his wife the same way.

You see, the husband aimed his verbal missile at his wife, but tiny bits of shrapnel pierced the soul of his son. And that's how it always is with anger.

Right now, you may think your anger is serving a valuable purpose. You may think it's causing the people in your life to be more obedient or submissive or productive. You may have become a master at motivating people through intimidation. But are you also hurting them?

Are you destroying their self-esteem?

Are you taking the joy out of their work?

Are you sending them home angry and discouraged?

Are you putting stress on their marriages?

Are you filling their hearts with hatred?

People who use anger as a tool can be very successful by the world's standards, but they always leave a trail of tears.

Fourth, anger stunts your spiritual growth. Years ago, I heard it said that you can never grow stronger than your biggest weakness. That's true in almost every area of life.

When Ozzie Smith first broke into the big leagues, he was a great fielder, but a terrible hitter. He was a 150-pound weakling who could barely hit the ball out of the infield. To his credit, he understood that his weakness as a hitter would ultimately cost him his job. So he went to work. He built up his body and studied the art of hitting like few men

> PEOPLE WHO USE ANGER AS A TOOL CAN BE VERY SUCCESSFUL BY THE WORLD'S STANDARDS, BUT THEY ALWAYS LEAVE A TRAIL OF TEARS.

ever have. He adapted his swing to fit his home ballpark and took thousands of hours of batting practice. To the amazement of many, he actually became a .300 hitter.

And now he's in the Hall of Fame.

He became great by turning his weakness into a strength.

If anger is your weakness, you must understand that it will keep you from ever becoming a strong Christian. It will poison virtually all your relationships. It will have you off chasing vengeance instead of the will of God. And it will ruin your witness. In short, it will turn you into a spiritual midget.

These are the reasons why you cannot simply live with your anger. So here's what I would suggest.

ATTACK YOUR ANGER

Attack it with confidence, knowing that it *can* be defeated. Yes, even the anger addict can be cured. Even the most deadly and deep-seated forms of anger can be driven out of a person's heart. How do I know? Because God said so in response to the first family squabble in history.

You may remember that Cain was hot under the collar because God rejected his sacrifice and accepted his brother's. That's when God, seeing trouble on the horizon, stepped in: "'Why are you so angry?' the LORD asked him. 'Why do you look so dejected? You will be accepted if you respond in the right way. But if you refuse to respond correctly, then watch out! Sin is waiting to attack and destroy you, and *you must subdue it*'" (Gen. 4:6–7, author's emphasis).

God made it clear that Cain's response to the situation would be of his own choosing. And so it is for all of us when we are angry and frustrated. We always have the choice of blowing our tops or keeping a lid on our anger. Even Proverbs 29:11 says, "A fool gives full vent to anger, but a wise person quietly holds it back."

If anger is a problem for you, let me suggest a plan of attack. Here are six things you can do that will help you get and keep your anger under control.

First, you can let God's Word become your counselor. Second Timothy 3:16 says, "All Scripture is inspired by God and is useful to teach us what is true and to make us realize what is wrong in our lives. *It straightens us out and teaches us to do what is right*" (author's emphasis).

Let me suggest that you start by studying the life of Christ. If ever a person was mistreated, it was Jesus. If ever a person was misunderstood, it was Jesus. If ever a person was let down by

His friends, it was Jesus. In other words, He had every reason to be one very angry man! But He wasn't. He was the kindest, gentlest man who's ever walked the face of the earth. Sure, there were times when He demonstrated what we might call righteous indignation. Sin and the effects of it drew some strong responses from Him. But he wasn't *known* for His anger, and He didn't live with a chip on His shoulder.

Go back and read the stories again, especially those surrounding the last week of His life. Notice the calm, reasoned responses to the hatred of His enemies. Notice the words of love and forgiveness that were spoken as He hung on the cross. Notice the incredible restraint He showed, even as ten thousand angels stood ready to swoop down and rescue Him from the cross.

There's an old hymn that says, "I stand amazed in the presence of Jesus, the Nazarene." You will too, my friend, if you'll simply open your Bible and take an honest look at Him. In a world that thrives on anger, the life of Christ will give you a clear example to follow.

Second, you can lower your expectations of people. One evening, just before the start of our midweek service, I felt a tug at my sleeve. Turning around, I found one of our faithful church ladies motioning for me to bend over so she could whisper something in my ear. I could tell by the look on her face that she was distressed, and I immediately thought I had done something to upset her. To my relief, I hadn't. Instead, she pointed to a young woman who had taken a seat on the aisle near the back of our auditorium. The young woman, who was a newcomer to our church, had kicked her shoes off and curled her feet up under her to get more comfortable. The lady was aghast, and whispered in my ear, "That's disgraceful! Please go over there and tell her she needs to show more respect to God's house!"

I took the lady by the arm and walked her a few feet farther away so we could talk more privately. I said, "I wholeheartedly agree with you that we should show respect to God's house. But you know something? That young lady is new to our church. She isn't even a Christian yet. She doesn't understand all the things you and I do about showing respect to the Lord. To be honest with you, I'm just so glad she's here that I don't care how she sits. In fact, if she wants to lie down, that's fine with me. I'd rather her be doing that than sitting on some bar stool. Why don't we just leave it alone and pray that God will use this Bible study to touch her heart?"

> WE GET FRUSTRATED AND ANGRY WHEN PEOPLE DON'T ACT THE WAY WE THINK THEY SHOULD, WITHOUT EVER STOPPING TO THINK THAT MAYBE THEY AREN'T CAPABLE.

The lady's anger melted away before my eyes. Her countenance brightened up and she said, "You're right. I'm going to pray for her."

Are you sometimes guilty of expecting Christian behavior out of people who aren't even Christians? Do you expect mature behavior out of people who are still babes in Christ? This is a common mistake. We get frustrated and angry when people don't act the way *we* think they should, without ever stopping to think that maybe they aren't capable.

One of my favorite passages of Scripture is Psalm 103:13–14. It says, "The LORD is like a father to his children, tender and compassionate to those who fear him. *For he understands how weak we are; he knows we are only dust*" (author's emphasis). The next time you feel yourself getting angry over someone else's failure, stop and remind yourself that we are all weak. Yes, even *you!*

Third, you can learn the difference between a mountain and a molehill. I have a little exercise I sometimes do with people in counseling sessions. When I encounter a person who's all bound up in anger and frustration, I pull out a notepad and pen and start making a list of all the things the person is upset about. Believe it or not, there have been times when the list was two or three pages long!

And then we start down the list, identifying each item as either a mountain or a molehill. A mountain is a matter of grave importance where the health and well-being of people or the cause of Christ hangs in the balance. A molehill, on the other hand, is a matter of lesser importance where, even if the worst were to happen, the damage done would be minimal and short-term.

> YOU SIMPLY CAN'T HELP BUT BE CRABBY WHEN YOU TURN EVERY LITTLE MOLEHILL INTO A GREAT BIG MOUNTAIN.

In all the years I've been doing this exercise, the counselee and I have always been able to identify more than half of the items on our list as molehills. In fact, there have been many times when we've been able to mark every single item as a molehill!

And what do you think happens next?

The counselee invariably walks out the door with a huge burden of anger and frustration lifted. Maybe it's not totally gone, but we've usually made a major dent in it.

Jesus talked about the Pharisees straining their water so they wouldn't accidentally swallow a gnat (Matt. 23:24). I've known people like that, and they're all grouchy and irritable, just like the Pharisees were. You simply can't help but be crabby when you turn every little molehill into a great big mountain.

Fourth, you can work at developing patience. Check out this little parable Jesus told. It's one of His more obscure ones, but it really speaks to this issue.

> A man planted a fig tree in his garden and came again and again to see if there was any fruit on it, but he was always disappointed. Finally, he said to his gardener, "I've waited three years, and there hasn't been a single fig! Cut it down. It's taking up space we can use for something else."
>
> The gardener answered, "Give it one more chance. Leave it another year, and I'll give it special attention and plenty of fertilizer. If we get figs next year, fine. If not, you can cut it down." (Luke 13:6–9)

In this parable we see a man who was angry and a man who wasn't. The difference in the two men is that one had patience and the other didn't.

I can attest to the fact that a lack of patience ultimately leads to anger. Most of my own angry outbursts over the years have been the result of pure impatience. I'm sure it was people just like me who invented supersonic flight, instant pudding, and microwave popcorn. I'm the kind of guy who wants it done yesterday, and when it doesn't happen, I get frustrated.

Our church recently relocated to a new facility four miles from our original location. When we first voted to make the move, experts estimated that the process might take two years to complete. That seemed like a long time, but I told myself I could handle it. In the end, it didn't take two years—it took five.

There were times when I wanted to pull what little hair I have left right out of my head. But now, looking back, I wonder if God didn't slow the whole project down just to teach me a lesson in patience. If He did, it worked. I've grown in that area. Nowadays I don't get as upset when things drag out.

How much less would your blood boil if you could learn to slow down? How many fewer tantrums would you throw if you could take life as it comes instead of trying to rush everything?

Fifth, you can resist the temptation to speculate. Too often, instead of taking words at face value, we overanalyze them. We try to read between the lines. We hear a statement and immediately wonder what the speaker *really* meant.

I have often made this mistake. Not long ago a sweet lady in our church approached me after one of our services. She complimented me on my sermon and then said, "Please preach more Bible." At first, I thought she meant, "We can never get enough Bible," which I totally agree with. But as the day wore on, that comment haunted me. The more I thought about it, the more I wondered what she was *really* saying. Was she implying that I am not a solid Bible preacher? Does she think my sermons are all fluff? Or pop psychology?

The first thing you know, an angry spirit was boiling in my heart. It wasn't until I shared the incident and my feelings with my wife that I was able to get myself straightened out. Marilyn helped me see how silly I was being. The lady in question was one of the nicest people we knew and had never been known to speak a harsh or unkind word. Yet, there I was turning her comment into something sinister.

If you also have this tendency, you need to memorize and live by Paul's words in Philippians 4:8. He said, "Fix your thoughts on what is true and honorable and right. Think about things that are pure and lovely and admirable. Think about things that are excellent and worthy of praise."

Sixth, you can loosen your grip on money. Paul wasn't joking when he said, "The love of money is at the root of all kinds of evil" (1 Tim. 6:10). I honestly can't think of anything that causes more anger and hard feelings. In fact, one of the more violent parables Jesus told has people making threats and even choking each other over money (Matt. 18:23–35). And every day on the news we hear about shootings and stabbings that are motivated by greed.

If ever there was a passage that Christians in our money-mad generation need to catch hold of, it's Proverbs 30:8–9: "Give me neither poverty nor riches! Give me just enough to satisfy my needs. For if I grow rich, I may deny you and say, 'Who is the LORD?' And if I am too poor, I may steal and thus insult God's holy name."

I can honestly say that the happiest people I know are not the poorest people I know, or the richest. They are the people in the middle, the people who have enough, but not too much. They're happier because they have fewer resentments, fewer worries, fewer debts, and fewer debtors. In short, they have fewer reasons to be angry.

Please understand that the six suggestions I've just given you are not designed to drain you of all anger. Rather, they are intended to keep you from misusing anger. In their book *Anger Is a Choice*, Tim LaHaye and Bob Phillips share a wonderful story that shows how important it is to have *some* anger, but not too much.

The story concerns a ferocious lion that was the terror of the jungle. Anytime the nearby villagers would venture into the jungle, he would chase them and bite them if he could. Finally, the villagers were fed up and decided to consult a wise old owl for advice. The owl said, "Don't worry; I'll go talk some sense into the lion."

The owl explained to the lion that he was only hurting himself by chasing and biting the villagers. He was getting a very bad reputation and would soon have no friends at all. Then he would become very lonely. The lion, afraid of being lonely, apologized and promised never to bite anyone again.

Before long, the villagers were venturing back into the jungle. At first, they were very careful around the lion. But when they saw that he had truly changed his ways, they began to lose their fear. They made faces at him as they walked by. They stuck out their tongues. They called him names and threw rocks at him. Then they took sticks and beat him.

One day the wise old owl came to visit the lion and found him in a cave, bruised and bleeding. The owl said, "What happened to you?" And the lion answered, "I promised you I wouldn't chase or bite the villagers, but now they're chasing me and throwing rocks at me and beating me."

The wise old owl said, "I told you not to chase or bite the villagers, but I didn't tell you not to roar!"

And so it is that in this chapter I'm not telling you to let people walk all over you. There are times and places when anger is perfectly justified. I'm simply saying that, as a strong man, there will always be a temptation to flex your muscles and show people who's boss. Like the lion, you may find yourself roaring and biting simply because you can, because it makes you feel like the tough guy you are, and because it gets quick results.

> REMEMBER, TRUE STRENGTH IS SEEN NOT IN THE ABILITY TO WREAK HAVOC AND DESTRUCTION, BUT IN THE ABILITY TO SHOW RESTRAINT.

But remember, true strength is seen not in the ability to wreak havoc and destruction, but in the ability to show restraint. Proverbs 16:32 says, "It is better to be patient than powerful; it is better to have self-control than to conquer a city."

SEVEN

STRONG MEN TEND TO REPEAT THE SAME MISTAKES

Sometimes our mouths and reactions operate before our brains get synchronized. That happens to me a lot.

—MIKE DITKA

Who will free me from this life that is dominated by sin? Thank God! The answer is in Jesus Christ our Lord.

—PAUL THE APOSTLE (ROMANS 7:24–25)

IT WAS THE NINTH INNING AND THE GAME WAS ON THE line. The score was tied with two outs. The bases were loaded. The crowd was on its feet.

Stepping into the box was a good hitter who was long over-due. Three times he had struck out and three times he had been caught looking. *Not this time,* he told himself. *This time I'm going to be aggressive. This time the pitcher's going to pay.*

He dug in and gave the pitcher his best game face. He took a couple of practice swings and settled into his stance. The muscles in his forearms flexed as the bat waggled behind his head. *He doesn't want to fall behind on the count. He's going to challenge me with a fastball.*

But the first pitch was a curve that painted the outside corner.

"Steeeerike one!" the umpire bellowed, as the crowd groaned.

The batter stepped out and took a deep breath. *OK, he tricked me. No problem. It only takes one swing. At least now I know he's going to throw a curve. He's ahead on the count and he just proved that he doesn't want to throw me a fastball if he doesn't have to.*

But the second pitch was indeed a blazing fastball, this time on the inside corner.

"Steeeerike two!" the umpire screamed.

The batter grimaced and walked away from the plate. He adjusted his helmet, tugged at his sleeve, and kicked at the dirt. Then he dug back in and took a practice swing. *He's gonna waste one. There's no way he's going to throw one over the plate with an 0-2 count. He wants me to go fishing, to get myself out on a ball that's six inches outside.*

But the next pitch was another blazing fastball, right down the middle.

The umpire whirled on his heel and threw a wicked overhand right into the cool night air. "Steeeerike three!"

Game over.

Boos rained down on the batter as he spun away from the plate in anger. Without thinking, he flung the bat high into the air and then jerked his helmet off and slammed it on the ground.

Bad move, as Sir Isaac Newton would have been quick to point out.

The bat flew about ten feet into the air and then came spinning back to earth like a propeller. The business end hit the batter squarely on top of the head and knocked him out cold.

The next day the batter was asked what was worse, getting caught looking with the game on the line or knocking himself out with the bat. His answer was a good one. He said, "That's easy. The bat deal was just one of those freaky things that could happen to anybody. But getting called out was much worse because I'd already done it three times. I knew I couldn't let it happen again, but I did. How many times does a guy have to screw up before he learns his lesson?"

Now, there's a question for the ages if I ever heard one.

In fact, it's the very question I find myself asking every time I read Samson's story. Wouldn't you think that after his brief but disastrous marriage to the girl from Timnah, he would have seen the light? Doesn't it seem logical that, after she nagged him unmercifully and betrayed him in the matter of the riddle, he would have realized that their relationship had been doomed from the very beginning? I mean, seriously, I can see him walking away saying, "Boy, Mom and Dad were right. Looks aren't everything. I never should have married that girl."

But no. Not our boy, Samson.

Instead, he did the unthinkable.

He went to her house to try to patch things up (Judg. 15:1). He even took along a goat to give her as a present, which, while not quite as aromatic as a bouquet of flowers and a box of chocolates, would have had considerable value in that culture.

Even as we see him trudging up to her front door with the goat in tow, we know that he's heading back into trouble. We want to scream, "Samson, what do you think you're doing? Can't you see that it's never going to work with that girl? How many times do you have to get burned before you learn your lesson?"

Interestingly, this is not the only time Samson repeated the same mistake. He continually associated himself with Philistine women and eventually allowed Delilah to nag him into revealing the secret of his strength just like his little Timnah beauty nagged him into revealing the answer to his riddle.

Does this part of Samson's story have an all-too-familiar ring to it? Would honesty compel you to admit that you, too, have made certain mistakes over and over again? Sometimes we call them "besetting sins." They are weaknesses that just seem to nag us throughout our lives and keep us from reaching our full potential.

I know a preacher who is extremely gifted. He's intelligent, visionary, personable, and a wonderful orator. And he loves the Lord with all his heart. But he's never held a ministry more than two or three years because he's never learned to control his tongue. James 3:5 says, "The tongue is a small thing, but what enormous damage it can do." This guy is a perfect example. He always manages to sabotage his ministries by being too blunt and outspoken. One person who was on the receiving end of one of his tirades told me that his words felt like karate chops. It takes him a couple of years, but he eventually manages to "karate chop" enough people in the congregation that he has no choice but to pack up and move on. It's my belief that if he could just get a handle on that one weakness and quit making that one mistake, the sky would be the limit of his potential.

Maybe you've had a similar experience. Maybe you've got all the skills you need to be very successful, and have even tasted success at various times, but have somehow managed to mess things up sooner or later. Maybe you've bounced from company to company or from marriage to marriage and, looking back, you can see that it's always the same mistakes that do you in.

THE REASONS

It's always important to understand what's at the heart of a problem before you try to solve it. I believe there are four reasons why strong, capable men make the same mistakes again and again.

First, even the strongest men are still human. Paul, one of the all-time great strong men, was brutally honest about his own feet of clay in Romans 7:16–18:

> I know perfectly well that what I am doing is wrong, and
> my bad conscience shows that I agree that the law is good.
> But I can't help myself, because it is sin inside me that
> makes me do these evil things. I know I am rotten through
> and through so far as my old sinful nature is concerned.
> No matter which way I turn, I can't make myself do right.
> I want to, but I can't.

We all know that feeling. We all understand the struggle he's talking about because we live it every day.

Not long ago I conducted a little experiment with myself. I was all alone in my office at about 8:00 A.M., praying for the day ahead. Having messed up a few times the day before, I decided I was going to make an extra effort to be good. I told myself that I was going to approach every situation with the kind of spiritual insight and maturity one would expect from a man in my position. I made up my mind that I was going to do my very best to get through the entire day without doing anything to disappoint God.

I lasted exactly thirty-seven minutes.

At 8:37 someone called with what I considered to be a whiny, silly complaint. I was nice on the phone, but when I hung up I was thoroughly exasperated and had some very unchristian thoughts pass through my mind. I was mumbling under my breath when, suddenly, I remembered my commitment. I glanced at my watch and saw that not even an hour had passed. I felt awful.

The truth is: I should have known better. The very thought that I could muster up the power to be good is ridiculous. Paul nailed it when he said, "I can't make myself do right. I want to, but I can't." That's why we need a Savior. If we could deal with the sin problem on our own we wouldn't need Jesus. Even the strongest men are still human and are going to stumble.

EVEN THE STRONGEST MEN ARE STILL HUMAN AND ARE GOING TO STUMBLE.

Second, many strong men have blind spots. In other words, they have weaknesses that they cannot see or do not recognize. David was acknowledging this reality in Psalm 139:23–24 when he said, "Search me, O God, and know my heart; test me and know my thoughts. *Point out anything in me that offends you,* and lead me along the path of everlasting life" (author's emphasis).

David knew all about blind spots because there was a time when one of his almost got a bunch of people killed. David and his men were living in the wilderness of Maon and were hungry. Nearby was a wealthy landowner named Nabal. They could have raided Nabal's estate and taken whatever they wanted, but instead David sent a ten-man delegation to kindly and respectfully ask for some supplies. Not only did Nabal refuse to give them any, but he also insulted David and his men by calling them a band of outlaws (1 Sam. 25:11).

When David heard this, he lost his cool. He strapped on his sword and ordered four hundred of his men to do the same. If Nabal thought they were outlaws, then outlaws they would be.

They would raid the estate, skewer Nabal on the end of a sword, and take whatever they wanted. It was going to be a bloodbath.

But Abigail saved the day.

Abigail was Nabal's wife. The Bible says she was a beautiful and sensible woman. Sensible enough to see what all the muscle-bound macho men in her world were not seeing. Quickly, she packed up some supplies without her husband's knowledge and went out to meet David. In a show of humility, she bowed before him and apologized for her husband's idiotic behavior. And then she said an amazing thing:

> Don't let this be a blemish on your record. Then you won't
> have to carry on your conscience the staggering burden of
> needless bloodshed and vengeance. (1 Sam. 25:31)

Suddenly, the blinders fell of off David's eyes. Suddenly, he could see that what he was about to do was terribly wrong. And this is what he said:

> Praise the LORD, the God of Israel, who has sent you to
> meet me today! Thank God for your good sense! Bless you
> for keeping me from murdering the man and carrying out
> vengeance with my own hands. (1 Sam. 25:32–33)

We all have blind spots. Unfortunately, we don't have an Abigail. We don't have someone who will tactfully point them out to us. And so we go right on making the same blunders again and again.

Third, many strong men have untended spiritual weaknesses. There's a striking phrase in Judges 15:1 that speaks volumes about Samson's motivation as he tried to salvage his relationship with the girl from Timnah. It says, "He intended to sleep with her." Of course, that was his motivation for marrying her in the first place, so nothing had changed. Samson's glaring weakness was in the area of sexuality and because he never dealt with it, he kept making the same mistakes over and over.

Fourth, many strong men have too much pride. I've mentioned this before, but here it comes into play again. When the riddle affair turned into an embarrassing fiasco resulting in the collapse of his marriage, it wounded his ego. Like many strong men today, he hated being thought of as a guy who couldn't hang on to his woman. In that culture, nothing would have been more humiliating. That's why he grabbed a goat, splashed on a little cologne, and made the journey to Ms. Timnah's house. The average person would have said, "Samson, can't you see she's not right for you?" But at that point he wasn't thinking about compatibility issues. His only concern was saving face. In this regard, Samson was like a boxer who gets knocked out by an inferior opponent. The first thing he does after he comes to is demand a rematch. His pride is wounded more than his body, and he can't wait for the chance to redeem himself.

THE REMEDY

Once you begin to solve the mystery of why you keep repeating the same mistakes, it's time to start thinking about how to stop. Let me offer you a four-step plan of action.

First, SIGN UP with a friend who will hold you accountable. One of the most striking things about Samson's story is that we never see him with a friend.

Lot had Abraham.

STRONG MEN TEND TO REPEAT THE SAME MISTAKES

Moses had Aaron.

Caleb had Joshua.

David had Jonathan.

Paul had Barnabas and Silas.

But Samson apparently didn't have anybody.

I read not long ago that over 85 percent of the violent crime victims in America are alone when they're attacked. That's not surprising. Bad guys know that their chances of pulling off a successful robbery or assault are much greater if the potential victim is isolated. Likewise, the Bible says that Satan prowls around looking for some victim to devour (1 Peter 5:8). That's *victim*, singular, not *victims*, plural.

Let me tell you about a man named Jack.

Jack worked with three other Christian guys in a small auto-repair shop. They shared devotions every Monday morning, attended the same church, and put forth a nice witness to the community through their business. But Jack loved big trucks and had always harbored a dream to drive over the road. One day, he got the opportunity. An acquaintance who knew of his desire called and offered him a job hauling cargo from coast to coast. He jumped at the chance.

The problem was that the job isolated him. No longer did he have his three Christian buddies by his side. Instead, he was stuck inside the cab of a truck for hours at a time, traveling to places where he wasn't known, and encountering temptations he wasn't accustomed to. It was the kind of freedom he'd never known but always longed for. It was liberating, fun, and exciting.

Until he got the news.

A girl he'd met at one of his stops was pregnant and claiming he was the father.

Jack's analysis of the situation was simple and painfully true. He said, "Looking back, I can see that the moment I struck out on my own, Satan showed up. He climbed right up into that cab with me, put his feet up on the dash, and made himself right at home. I never really knew what temptation was until I found myself all alone a thousand miles from home."

And that's how Satan works. He'll badger anybody, but he especially loves to pick on a man who's all alone.

So don't let it happen.

Don't make yourself an easy target.

Don't let yourself be caught without an accountability relationship.

Hook up with someone you can trust. Someone you can talk to about intimate things. Not a "yes man," but someone who cares enough about you to tell you the truth, even if it hurts. Hook up with someone who will point out your blind spots. Hook up with someone who will get in your face if necessary to keep you from doing something self-destructive. Proverbs 27:6 says, "Wounds from a friend are better than many kisses from an enemy." And verse 17 of the same chapter says, "As iron sharpens iron, a friend sharpens a friend."

Second, GIVE UP your rationalizations. A lot of guys know very well that they are complicating their lives by making the same mistakes again and again, but instead of changing, they simply shrug and say, "I can't help it. That's just the way God made me." I can just imagine Samson's response to anyone who might have questioned his promiscuous lifestyle. He would have said, "What can I say? I've got a strong sex drive. A man's gotta do what a man's gotta do!" Of course, this attitude is nothing new. Since Adam in the Garden of Eden, men have been rationalizing their bad behavior.

If that's what you've been doing, let me challenge you to stop it.

Quit lying to yourself and others.

Quit pretending to be a victim.

Quit acting as though you're helpless.

Instead, start claiming the power and freedom you have in Christ. Listen to what Paul said in Colossians 2:13–15:

> You were dead because of your sins and because your sinful nature was not yet cut away. Then God made you alive with Christ. He forgave all our sins. He canceled the record that contained the charges against us. He took it and destroyed it by nailing it to Christ's cross. In this way, *God disarmed the evil rulers and authorities.* He shamed them publicly by his victory over them on the cross of Christ (author's emphasis).

Did you catch that? It says, "God disarmed the evil rulers and authorities." That means he took away their weapons. He eliminated their power to control you. He fixed it so you don't have to be afraid of them anymore.

And then verse 20 of the same chapter says it again: "You have died with Christ, and *he has set you free from the evil powers of this world*" (author's emphasis).

After reading these verses, can't you see how silly it is for any Christian to plead helplessness in the face of sin? It doesn't matter how long you've had a bad habit or how many times you've made the same mistake, you can change because the evil rulers and authorities have been disarmed. You've been set free from their power! Granted, this won't be easy. But if God's Word is true, it *is* possible.

It's time to give up your lame excuses.

Third, LINE UP your life with God's Word. When I was a kid, it was my job to put the chalk lines on the field at our local ball diamond. I'll never forget the first time I did it. I had been told to stretch a string from the back corner of home plate to the outfield grass and line it up perfectly with the foul pole. Then I could push the chalk dispenser right along the string and make a nice straight line. But that seemed like a lot of extra work to me. I didn't think I needed the string. I just knew I could make a straight line simply by eyeballing it.

You can guess what happened.

I wrinkled up my brow in concentration and started pushing the dispenser in what felt like a perfectly straight line. I was so very careful not to veer off line. But when I got to first base and turned around to inspect my work, it was a mess! The baseline I had made was so crooked it looked like a graph of the Dow Jones Industrials!

Friend, the only way for you to keep from repeatedly veering off in the Christian life is to stretch out the string of God's Word and then follow it. If you try to eyeball a situation or follow your feelings, you'll get off track every time.

In Scripture, Solomon was a strong man who made this mistake. Instead of stretching out the string of God's Word and following it, he eyeballed difficult situations and acted on his feelings. He did whatever seemed prudent from a human point of view. That's how he became the all-time champ, the world-record holder, the undisputed king of repeated mistakes. We know for a fact that he made the same mistake 699 times because the Bible says he had 700 wives (1 Kings 11:3)! Wouldn't you think that somewhere along the line—maybe at about wife number 50—Solomon would have figured out that he was veering off track? But he didn't, and that just goes to show you how unreliable man's judgment is.

How ironic it is that Solomon was the one who instructed us not to try to eyeball our ways through life. He said, "Trust in the LORD with all your heart; *do not depend on your own understanding*. Seek his will in all you do, and he will direct your paths" (Proverbs 3:5–6, author's emphasis). If anyone knew the wisdom of those words, Solomon did.

Fourth, POWER UP with the Holy Spirit. One of the greatest things about reading and studying the Old Testament is that you get to see in such graphic terms how God empowers His people and enables them to overcome even the most intimidating foes. Samson is a case in point. Again and again we read about the Spirit of the Lord powerfully taking control of him (Judges 14:6, 15:19, 15:14). With that power working through him he ripped a lion's jaws apart and even killed a thousand men with the jawbone of a donkey (15:15). The sad thing is that Samson never employed that same Holy Spirit power in the battle against temptation.

But just because *he* didn't, doesn't mean *you* can't.

Listen to Romans 8:1–2:

> So now there is no condemnation for those who belong to Christ Jesus. *For the power of the life-giving Spirit has freed you through Christ Jesus from the power of sin that leads to death* (author's emphasis).

And then verse 6 of the same chapter:

> If your sinful nature controls your mind, there is death. But if the Holy Spirit controls your mind, there is life and peace.

And, finally, verses 12 and 13:

> So, dear brothers and sisters, you have no obligation what-
> soever to do what your sinful nature urges you to do. For if
> you keep on following it, you will perish. But if *through the*
> *power of the Holy Spirit* you turn from it and its evil deeds,
> you will live (author's emphasis).

Paul was writing these words to real people, just like you and me, who were battling those nagging, besetting sins. His message is simple: You have a sinful nature that works against you, but God's Spirit is more powerful. *He* will be the secret of your success. Yes, it's important to hook up with a friend, to give up your rationalizations, and to line up your life with God's Word. But even those measures will ultimately fail if you don't tap into the Holy Spirit's power.

The way to do that is by emptying yourself of all pride and surrendering completely to the Lord, which I'll talk more about in the next chapter. You see, the Spirit can't fill what's already full. If you're trusting your own strength to deal with the temptations of life, God can't help you. It's only when you humble yourself before God and admit that you can't do it on your own that He will lift you up. Read these words from James very carefully:

> What do you think the Scriptures mean when they say that
> the Holy Spirit, whom God has placed within us, jealously
> longs for us to be faithful? He gives us more and more
> strength to stand against such evil desires. As the Scriptures
> say, "God sets himself against the proud, but he shows
> favor to the humble." (4:5–6)

As I come to the conclusion of this chapter, I'm reminded of an observation an elderly preacher once made about the church he was serving. He said, "Our problem is simple. We have too many oxymorons in our church."

Puzzled, I asked what he meant.

He said, "An oxymoron is a contradiction in terms, like when you say that somebody is *pretty ugly*, or when you talk about going on a *working vacation*. In our church, we have too many *sinful Christians*. We have too many Christians who claim to love the Lord, but have never gotten serious about cleaning up their lives."

That's blunt, isn't it? But it's a statement worth thinking about.

Are *you* an oxymoron?

Are you a Christian who's never gotten serious about cleaning up your life?

Have you never taken dead aim on your besetting sin?

Are you still making the same blunders you were making years ago?

If so, I know you're as much of a disappointment to yourself as you are to God because there's never any joy in that kind of life. There wasn't for Samson and there will never be for you either. So why don't you make up your mind right now that you're going to escape this aspect of the Samson Syndrome once and for all?

SIGN UP with a friend who will hold you accountable.

GIVE UP your rationalizations.

LINE UP your life with God's Word.

And POWER UP with the Holy Spirit.

EIGHT

STRONG MEN TEND TO HAVE BIG EGOS

Many times at the beach a good-looking lady will say to me, "I want to touch you." I always smile and say, "I don't blame you."

—ARNOLD SCHWARZENEGGER

Not to us, O LORD, but to you goes all the glory.

—PSALM 115:1

I WAS BORN AND RAISED IN ILLINOIS. I READ RECENTLY that my home state gets its name from an Indian word to which a French suffix was added. The word means "a tribe of superior men." I've not found Illinois residents to be superior, but whoever came up with that name must have thought otherwise. My guess is that the person was a strong man. Strong men tend to think very highly of themselves.

Take Samson, for example.

In Judges 15:8 we find him living in a cave, not out of fear, but simply because he'd been slaughtering Philistines right and left and needed a place to rest. At the same time, the Philistines were conducting raids against the people of Judah. Their goal was to smoke Samson out of his hiding place and take him into custody. Naturally, the leaders of Judah were concerned about their own survival, so they decide to capture Samson themselves and turn him over to the Philistines. Anything to get the Philistines off their backs.

Judges 15:11 says that three thousand men went after Samson. That seems a little bit like swatting a mosquito with a sledgehammer, doesn't it? You would think that no more than a dozen men would be needed to capture one individual, but Samson's reputation as a warrior had grown to such an extent that normal procedures seemed woefully inadequate. He'd spilled gallons of Philistine blood without receiving so much as a scratch, so the men of Judah were taking no chances.

However, in a surprise move, Samson gave up without a fight. He even allowed himself to be tied up when the men of Judah promised they wouldn't kill him. Of course, they should have guessed that he was playing possum. They should have known that he would never allow himself to be turned over to the dreaded Philistines. But apparently, it didn't occur to them. Instead, they came marching into the village of Lehi with Samson in tow, believing they had finally solved their problem. With Samson under wraps, the Philistines would stop raiding their villages and they could finally live in peace.

And that's when it happened.

As the Philistines were dancing in the streets, the Spirit of the Lord once again took hold of Samson. He flexed his muscles and the ropes that bound him snapped like dried-up vines. Suddenly, the prancing turned to pandemonium. Samson was like a wild animal that had broken out of its cage. He had no weapon, but found the jawbone of a donkey lying at his feet. As women grabbed their children and ran for cover, Samson picked up the jawbone and turned to face the Philistine soldiers who were drawing their swords and deploying in battle formation.

What happened next is one of the most amazing feats in the Bible. With nothing in his hands but a donkey's dentures, Samson slaughtered a thousand Philistines. No doubt they came at him from every direction, swinging swords and flashing armor, but with the Spirit of the Lord empowering him, he was equal to the task. When all was said and done, the countryside was littered with bodies and the dirt was soaked with Philistine blood.

What an opportunity that was for Samson to set his life on a better course. If only he had fallen on his face and acknowledged the Lord's hand in his victory. If only he had felt compelled to thank God for sparing his life, perhaps he could have gotten back on track spiritually and the second half of his life would have been different. But it didn't happen. Instead, he spontaneously composed a poem about his amazing accomplishment. A poem that speaks volumes about his character. We see it in Judges 15:16:

> With the jawbone of a donkey,
> I've made heaps on heaps!
> With the jawbone of a donkey,
> I've killed a thousand men!

Without God's help, Samson would undoubtedly have been killed. But his little "ditty" contains not one word about God. Not one word of acknowledgment. Not one word of gratitude. Instead, he takes all the glory for himself.

Sickening, isn't it?

But wait a minute.

Before we hammer Samson, we better take a look at ourselves. It's very common for strong men to have big egos. You can see it in superstar athletes who pout like children if they aren't paid megamillions of dollars. You can see it in corporate big shots who treat their subordinates like second-class citizens. You can see it in salesmen who live beyond their means just to project an image of success. You can see it in husbands who grow insecure when their wives' achievements exceed their own. You can hear it in the conversations of men who think they know everything. And you can even see it in preachers and missionaries who exaggerate the success of their ministries.

> PRIDE HAS BEEN THE MOTIVATION FOR SOME OF THE GREATEST ATROCITIES IN HISTORY, INCLUDING THE HOLOCAUST.

A lot of people believe pride is a minor, rather harmless sin. Years ago I saw a survey in which Christians were asked to rank a variety of sins according to their seriousness. Pride didn't even make the top ten. That's because most people tend to see pride as more of an annoyance than a full-blown sin. We think it makes people irritating and obnoxious, but not dangerous. However, history says otherwise. Pride has been the motivation for some of the greatest atrocities in history, including the Holocaust. It was Hitler's belief in the superiority of the Aryan race that powered the Nazi war machine and put an estimated six million European Jews to death between 1939 and 1945.

Another indication of the deadly seriousness of the sin of pride is the Bible's complete condemnation of it. Consider the following verses:

There are six things the Lord hates—no, seven things he detests: *haughty eyes*, a lying tongue, hands that kill the innocent, a heart that plots evil, feet that race to do wrong, a false witness who pours out lies, a person who sows discord among brothers. (Prov. 6:16–19, author's emphasis)

The LORD despises pride; be assured that the proud will be punished. (Prov. 16:5)

Haughty eyes, a proud heart, and evil actions are all sin. (Prov. 21:4)

I, the LORD, will punish the world for its evil and the wicked for their sin. I will crush the arrogance of the proud and the haughtiness of the mighty. (Isa. 13:11)

"See, I am your enemy, O proud people," says the Lord, the LORD Almighty. "Your day of reckoning has arrived. O land of pride, you will stumble and fall, and no one will raise you up." (Jer. 50:31–32)

YOUR PERCH ON THE
PEDESTAL OF PRIDE

Right now, you may be wondering if you've fallen prey to this aspect of the Samson Syndrome. You may be a strong, gifted man with healthy self-esteem and a lot of self-confidence. You may be driving a car you can barely afford. You may have a closet full of designer clothes. You may be dating a woman, not because you love her, but because she looks good on your arm and makes other men envious. And now, after reading the first part of this chapter, you may be wondering if you've crossed the line. You may be wondering if God views you as a haughty individual. It's an important question that I believe you can answer simply by taking a close look at Samson. His life teaches us several things about life on the pedestal of pride.

First, on the pedestal of pride there is an absence of heartfelt worship. This is one of the most striking things about Samson's life. He was handpicked by God, raised by righteous parents who loved the Lord, and shaped in his formative years according to the disciplines of the Nazirite vow, yet not once do we see any indication that he had a meaningful devotional life. Not once do we see him worshiping the Lord. Not once do we hear him singing praises. As far as we know, he didn't even pray unless he was in desperate trouble.

THE REASON PROUD PEOPLE RARELY WORSHIP IS BECAUSE WORSHIP IS, ULTIMATELY, AN ACT OF HUMILITY.

The reason proud people rarely worship is because worship is, ultimately, an act of humility. When you bow before the Lord, you're acknowledging that He is greater than you are. You're confessing your weakness. You're admitting that you need His help. Proud people just have a hard time doing that.

However, that doesn't mean you won't find proud people in church. On the contrary, proud people often flock to church because it's such a great place to get their egos fed. They can show off their new outfits, display their musical talents, demonstrate their wisdom in a Sunday-school class, or even assume positions of leadership. It's interesting to note that the most ego-driven people of Jesus' day were the Pharisees, who were the leaders of the Jewish religion.

Here's the point:

Pride and *religion* often go together.

But pride and *worship* never do.

So if you want to know if you have a problem in this area, here's the first question you should ask yourself: Do you truly have a heart for worship?

Second, on the pedestal of pride there is foolishness. I find it interesting that Samson's ego got bigger and bigger as time went along, and so did the foolish risks he was willing to take. It's almost as if he was just asking to be humiliated. And of course, he was, eventually.

Proverbs 16:18 says, "Pride goes before destruction, and haughtiness before a fall." And Proverbs 17:19 says, "Anyone who speaks boastfully invites disaster." I think about that last verse every time I hear a high-profile athlete boasting to the press.

Like Warren Sapp.

Before the 2001–2002 NFL season, the supertalented All-Pro defensive lineman for the Tampa Bay Buccaneers predicted that he would set the single-season sack record. He was in his prime and coming off of a great year in which he recorded 16.5 sacks, so it seemed like a real possibility. By season's end, a new sack record (22.5) had been set—but by Michael Strahan, not Warren Sapp. Warren's measly total of six was considered an embarrassment in light of his foolish prediction.

> PRIDE AND RELIGION OFTEN GO TOGETHER. BUT PRIDE AND WORSHIP NEVER DO.

"Anyone who speaks boastfully invites disaster."

Why is this true? Probably for two reasons. First, because boastful people tend to rile up their competition. When you brag about what you're going to do, you can bet someone's going to get fired up and try extrahard to stop you. But also, boastful people face opposition from God. James 4:6 says, "God sets himself against the proud, but he shows favor to the humble." Anytime you go into an endeavor with God set against you, your chances of failure are increased.

Think back over the years of your life. Would you be forced to admit that your ego has compelled you to do some pretty foolish things?

Third, on the pedestal of pride there is isolation. I mentioned in the last chapter that Samson apparently had no close friends. But here we see an even more striking illustration of his isolation: He was hiding out in a cave, and even his own people were turning against him. There appeared to not be a single individual who was on his side!

Is it enough just to say that Samson was a loner and didn't want to get close to people? I don't think so. It's much more likely that he had the kind of personality that drove people away. Strong men with big egos are always intimidating. They radiate power and authority like heat from a furnace. They can make you feel inferior. They can make you afraid to speak your mind. They can have you backpedaling and apologizing even when you haven't done anything wrong. And they are overbearing. If you've ever gotten trapped in a one-on-one conversation with a pretentious snob, you know that all too well. I sometimes wonder if the reason Samson spent so much time in the company of women was because he had such a hard time relating to men. Perhaps he longed for the kind of camaraderie that only two good male buddies can share, but was never able to find it. So he settled for sex.

Are there times when you feel isolated? Does it often seem as though the whole world is against you? Do your relationships seem shallow and surfacy? If so, could it be that your ego is killing potential friendships?

Fourth, on the pedestal of pride there is disappointment. Way back in 1927, Babe Ruth hit his sixtieth home run off of Tom Zachary of the Washington Senators. After the game he pranced around the Yankee clubhouse yelling, "Count 'em. Sixty! Let's see somebody match that!"

Well, it took a while, but Roger Maris eventually did it. With one swing of the bat, the Babe's record was significantly diminished.

And that's why there's always disappointment on the pedestal of pride. Whatever the source of your pride, it's bound to be temporary. If you take pride in your handsome appearance, just wait; wrinkles are on their way. If you take pride in your athletic ability, just wait; arthritis is coming. If you take pride in your business savvy, just wait; a brilliant young hotshot has just applied for a job with your company. And if you take great pride in your cleverness, as Samson did, just wait; there's bound to be a Delilah in your future, someone who'll come along and outsmart you. No wonder Proverbs 29:23 says, "Pride ends in humiliation."

Right now would be a great time for you to look back and see how many times you've felt disappointed or even humiliated because somebody managed to surpass or outperform you. The Bible says we should rejoice with others in their successes (Rom. 12:15). Are you able to do that? Or do you feel threatened when good things happen to other people?

YOUR HOPE FOR A
HEART OF HUMILITY

If you're starting to realize that you have a problem with pride, that's definitely a step in the right direction. A good second step would be to get a picture of true humility firmly implanted in your mind as a point of reference. The Bible offers many, but one of the best is in Acts 14.

Paul and Barnabas were doing evangelistic work in Lystra. One day, while Paul was preaching, he noticed a man in the audience that he knew had been lame from birth. Somehow, Paul sensed that the man had great faith and told him to stand up. You can imagine the crowd leaning forward, watching in amazement as the man struggled to his feet, found his balance, and started walking around without help.

That's all it took.

The people exploded in celebration and the news began to spread through the city like wildfire. Eyewitnesses were telling everyone they met that Paul and Barnabas were gods in human bodies. Don't ask me how, but they actually came to the conclusion that Barnabas was Zeus and Paul was Hermes. They even ran home to gather up oxen and flowers so they could offer them as sacrifices to the apostles at the city gates (Acts 14:8–13).

What an opportunity that was for Paul and Barnabas! If they'd had any kind of business sense at all (or at least a good agent), they could have capitalized on their sudden celebrity status in a big way. They could have run for office and won. They could have had servants rushing to do their bidding. They could have had beautiful women at their beck and call.

Instead, they threw it all away with these words:

Friends, why are you doing this? We are merely human

beings like yourselves! We have come to bring you the Good News that you should turn from these worthless things to the living God, who made heaven and earth, the sea, and everything in them. (Acts 14:15)

I see in those words the cure for sinful pride. It's a simple, three-step process.

First, remember what you are. Paul and Barnabas said, "We are merely human beings like yourselves!"

Shaquille O'Neal is easily the most dominating player in the NBA. He possesses a combination of size, strength, speed, and agility that is unlike anything sports fans have ever seen. Perhaps it's no wonder that he has the Superman insignia tattooed on his body and that he uses it as a kind of personal logo. No one would deny that Shaq is a superphysical specimen. But is he Superman? Apparently not, because recently he was forced to miss several games with an arthritic toe. Supermen don't have arthritis.

By contrast, think about Wayne Gretzky. With stats that are truly mind-boggling and almost sixty NHL records in his hip pocket, he was, arguably, the greatest hockey player ever to lace up a pair of skates. Consider that he won:

four Stanley Cups
nine Hart Memorial Trophies (season MVP)
two Conn Smythe Trophies (Stanley Cup MVP)
ten Art Ross Trophies (season scoring title)
five Lester B. Pearson Awards (outstanding player
    selected by NHL players)
four Lady Byng Memorial Trophies (most gentlemanly
    player).

Is it any wonder NHL fans call him The Great One?

But guess what.

You'll never hear Wayne Gretzky call *himself* The Great One. Nor will you find any Superman logos tattooed on his body. Rather, his attitude toward himself is summed up in a statement he made on ESPN's *Up Close* in 1996: "I'm more comfortable with people just calling me Wayne. There've been a couple of stretches in my career where I probably could have been called The Good One or The Mediocre One."

Isn't that refreshing? In a generation when so many superstar athletes have lost all perspective, isn't it nice to hear a truly great player use the word *mediocre* with reference to himself?

I believe the first step toward humility is to remember and acknowledge what you are. You are an imperfect human being. It doesn't matter how many records you've set or awards you've won. It doesn't matter how vast your worldly kingdom is or how high you've managed to climb on the ladder of success. There's no getting around the fact that you are made of dust, not steel, and someday, if the Lord tarries in His return, you are going to die. And when you do, the world won't skip a beat. It'll keep right on spinning without you.

> WHEN YOU THROW UP YOUR HANDS AND SCREAM, "I'M NOT SUPERMAN!" PRESSURE IS IMMEDIATELY RELIEVED.

These words may have a dismal ring to them, but I have a surprise for you: They are actually quite liberating. When you let them soak into your heart and take root, they'll actually begin to transform your life. You see, there's pressure in trying to be Superman. People are constantly tugging on your cape. They run straight to you when they have a problem. They expect you to fix everything and are disappointed when you can't. But when you throw up your hands and scream, "I'm not Superman!" pressure is immediately relieved.

My own experience has confirmed this. As a young preacher, I thought I had to *be* and *do* everything for the church I was serving. I foolishly believed that because I was a trained professional, I was the key to our success. As a result, I took the burden of every ministry on my shoulders. I served on every committee, attended every meeting, and fought every battle. Essentially, I set myself up to fail because there inevitably came a time when I reached the limit of my endurance. It was only when I gave up my Superman complex and learned to delegate responsibility that I was set free from a lot of that stress.

Always remember what you are.

Second, remember why you're here. I like the story about the depressed preacher who went for a walk in the woods. Without realizing it, he wandered close to a military installation. A sentry who was patrolling the perimeter raised his rifle and shouted, "Halt! Who are you and why are you here?" The preacher stopped and gave the sentry a puzzled look. "What did you say?" he asked. Again the sentry shouted, "Who are you and why are you here?" And with that, the preacher broke into a wide grin. He shook the sentry's hand and said, "Thank you so much for reminding me what I need to be thinking about."

The thing I love about Paul and Barnabas is that they never stopped thinking about who they were and why they were here. When the people showed a desire to worship them, they immediately admitted their humanity and restated their purpose. "We have come to bring you the Good News," they said (Acts 14:15).

It's easy for strong, proud men to forget why they're here. Strong men tend to get so caught up in the various competitions of life—whether it's for a job, a promotion, a woman, or a lifestyle—that they lose sight of a simple, basic truth: We were made to worship and serve our Creator. Jesus spoke forcefully to this issue in Mark 8:34–35:

> If any of you wants to be my follower, . . . you must put aside your selfish ambition, shoulder your cross, and follow me. If you try to keep your life for yourself, you will lose it. But if you give up your life for my sake and for the sake of the Good News, you will find true life.

And then He came up with two questions that seem perfectly aimed at strong men:

> And how do you benefit if you gain the whole world but lose your own soul in the process? Is anything worth more than your soul? (vv. 36–37)

I love this poem from an unknown author. It has helped me keep my own thinking straight.

> To have your name inscribed up there is greater yet by far,
> Than all the halls of fame down here and every man-
> made star.
> This crowd on earth, they soon forget the heroes of the
> past;
> They cheer like mad until you fall and that's how long
> you last.
> I tell you, friend, I would not trade my name, however
> small,
> If written there beyond the stars in that celestial hall.

> For any famous name on earth or glory that they share,
>
> I'd rather be an unknown here and have my name up
>
> there.

You may already be famous. Or maybe fame is in your future. Perhaps you'll win a chest full of medals or reach heights in your profession that no one has reached before. But if you don't, it's OK because your primary calling is simply to worship and serve your Creator. That's ultimately why you're here. If you can remember that as you go about your business, you will find what Jesus calls "true life," that is, a life of peace, joy, and purpose.

> STRONG MEN TEND TO GET SO CAUGHT UP IN THE VARIOUS COMPETITIONS OF LIFE . . . THAT THEY LOSE SIGHT OF A SIMPLE, BASIC TRUTH: WE WERE MADE TO WORSHIP AND SERVE OUR CREATOR.

Third, remember who you serve. Still in Acts 14:15, Paul and Barnabas said, "We have come to bring you the Good News that *you should turn from these worthless things to the living God*" (author's emphasis). Clearly, they never lost sight of whose kingdom they were trying to build.

Right now, whose kingdom are you trying to build?

Yours? Or God's?

In Scripture, Nehemiah is a man who stands out as a builder for God, and not surprisingly, it was his humility that propelled him to his greatest achievement. You see, he had a cushy job in the palace of the King of Persia. He was the king's cupbearer, or wine taster, which means he was the king's first line of defense against assassination by poisoning. On the surface, that might not sound like the greatest job in the world. But think about it. Only the most respected and trustworthy men could be allowed to hold such a position. So when the king found such a man, he took good care of him. Real good care. Nehemiah's life would have been very comfortable.

But one day Nehemiah heard a disturbing report about his people, the Jews. "Things are not going well for those who returned to the province of Judah. They are in great trouble and disgrace. The wall of Jerusalem has been torn down, and the gates have been burned" (Neh. 1:3). Nehemiah was so upset by this news that he mourned, fasted, and prayed for days.

During that time, Nehemiah was searching his own heart and trying to determine what, if anything, he should do. Should he stay put and go on living the good life? Maybe snag a promotion or two and work his way on up the ladder of power and prestige? Or should he give it all up and go to Jerusalem to try to help his people rebuild not only their city, but their souls as well?

I believe every strong Christian man will have what we could call a "Nehemiah moment" sooner or later. It's that moment when you come to a fork in the road. One way leads to comfort and the other leads to sacrifice. It's that moment when you have to decide whether you're going to serve yourself or your God. You have to choose between laying up treasures on earth or in heaven. You have to make up your mind whether you care more about *your* comfort or *His* kingdom.

It takes a humble guy to make the right choice.

A guy like Nehemiah.

He walked away from the good life to undertake an enormously difficult and dangerous project. A lot of people probably thought he was crazy. That's usually the conclusion people draw when they see someone give up the pleasures of the world to serve God. But he wasn't crazy. Not at all. He simply held to a view of things that placed God's interests above his own.

And that's humility.

One of my biggest prayers for this book is that it will bring many strong men to their "Nehemiah moments." In fact, I hope it's happening to you right now. I hope you're starting to see that there is a fork in the road in front of you. An alternative to the self-serving lifestyle the world encourages you to live. It may be a little uphill at times. It may appear to be leading off into a dark, unknown wilderness. But you have our Lord's promise that it is the road that leads to His richest blessings. That's what Jesus meant when He said, "The humble will be honored" (Luke 18:14).

Remember what you are.

Remember why you're here.

Remember who you serve.

Three simple steps that will lead you safely down from the pedestal of pride.

NINE

STRONG MEN TEND TO TAKE FOOLISH RISKS

If I miss the jump and hit the wall head-on, I'm just going to get somewhere quicker where you are all going someday. And I'm going to sit there and have a beer and wait for you.

—EVEL KNIEVEL

Fools are destroyed by their lack of common sense.

—SOLOMON (PROVERBS 10:21)

ON SEPTEMBER 8, 1974, ROBERT CRAIG KNIEVEL, BETTER known as Evel Knievel, did something that made him either the bravest human being on the planet, or the craziest. Or perhaps both. He climbed into a contraption called a "skycycle" with the intention of being launched from one side of the Snake River Canyon to the other. In order to accomplish the feat, he would need a two-hundred-foot ramp, five hundred pounds of thrust, and a takeoff speed of at least three hundred miles an hour.

Not even Evel himself believed he could make it.

Already two prototype, unmanned skycycles had been launched, with both failing miserably, falling into the deep gorge like a rock. After two years of research and testing, there was not one logical reason for Evel to attempt this stunt. Not one piece of evidence suggested he could be successful. Yet the world's greatest daredevil had been promising for seven years that he would do it, and he was going to. Or die trying.

He was lifted into Skycycle 3 by a crane. After he was strapped in, a priest walked up a ramp and gave him last rites. A high-school band played the national anthem. Then, in an extraordinary move, Bob Truax, the skycycle's engineer, went to Evel and begged him to call off the jump. He felt the wind was blowing too hard in the wrong direction. In truth, he knew Evel had no shot at being successful, wind or no wind. But Evel waved him away, passing up what he truly believed was the last exit ramp off of the freeway that was leading him to certain death.

Seconds later, with millions looking on around the world, Skycycle 3 roared to life as a blast of hot steam shot out of its tail. Then it began to move, picking up speed as it shot up the ramp. But about two-thirds of the way up the ramp, something happened that Evel's wife, Linda, still believes was an act of God and an answer to her prayers. The skycycle's parachute deployed. It didn't stop the rocket from being launched into midair, but it did enable the ill-fated projectile to float to the bottom of Snake River Canyon, where it landed safely on the riverbank. Ironically, the strong wind that appeared to be working against the jump might well have saved Evel's life, for it kept him from landing in the deepest part of the river, where he likely would have drowned.

Obviously, not every strong man has the guts and raw courage of Evel Knievel, but it's not at all unusual for strong men to carry on escapades that stretch the limits of good judgment.

Again, Samson is a case in point.

When we come to the first verse of Judges 16, we find him in a very dangerous situation. First, he's in Gaza, a Philistine city that was forty-five miles from his home in Zorah. Second, he's in bed with a prostitute, which, of course, was a serious offense before God. But beyond that, it was very risky. The woman was obviously a Philistine, and would have had no qualms about betraying him into the hands of her countrymen. In fact, though the text doesn't say so, we can assume she did just that, for we're told that the men of Gaza gathered that very night for the purpose of capturing Samson. It's likely that many of the prostitutes in that area had been told that Samson might come calling and were offered a sizable reward for information leading to his capture.

This particular section of Samson's story raises more questions than it answers. For example, we'd love to know how Samson was able to slip out of the woman's bed at midnight and make his way past the soldiers that had gathered to capture him. And even more to the point, why did he feel the need to get up and go? Was his conscience bothering him? Did the woman say something that aroused his suspicions? Was he hearing strange noises outside the bedroom window? These are things God chose not to reveal. Perhaps the reason is because they would have needlessly clouded the picture he most wanted us to see, that of a strong man taking a foolish risk.

I'm sure we would all agree that some risk taking is good. Risk takers defend our freedom, put out our fires, and take criminals off of our streets. Risk takers invest in new ideas that lead to life-changing advances in science and technology. Risk takers put up the money to start the businesses that add quality and convenience to our lives. Risk takers push the limits of the imagination and take us to wonderful places we've never been before in music, art, and literature.

I'm all in favor of risk taking!

As long as the risks aren't foolish.

CAN YOU THINK OF SOME OCCASIONS WHEN YOU RISKED YOUR HEALTH, YOUR REPUTATION, YOUR JOB, OR YOUR MARRIAGE IN A WAY THAT YOU LATER REALIZED MADE NO SENSE?

If you're a strong man, you've probably been known to stretch the limits of good judgment from time to time. Recently, a friend of mine told me that there have been at least a half dozen times in his life when he could have—and probably should have—died, simply because of his own stupidity.

Think back over your own life.

Can you recall a few of those times?

Can you think of some occasions when you risked your health, your reputation, your job, or your marriage in a way that you later realized made no sense?

And have those occasions been recent?

Do you have a habit of playing with fire?

If so, you're a victim of the Samson Syndrome and you need to get a handle on this aspect of your life. Proverbs 6:27–28 asks, "Can a man scoop fire into his lap and not be burned? Can he walk on hot coals and not blister his feet?" Of course, the answer is *no*.

Think about Evel Knievel again. Sure, he survived the Snake River Canyon fiasco and managed to walk away from the skycycle in good health. But over the course of his career he spent a total of thirty-six months in the hospital recovering from stunt-related injuries. He had fourteen surgeries to repair or replace broken bones, many with steel screws, pins or rods. And he broke over twenty different bones in his body, some as many as five different times.

You simply *can't* play with fire without getting burned.

FOUR KINDS OF RISKS

If you've been a foolish risk taker in the past, the first step to overcoming that tendency is to think carefully about risks in general. There are four different kinds.

First, there are UNAVOIDABLE RISKS. On March 16, 2002, thirteen-year-old Brittanie Cecil went to an NHL game in Columbus, Ohio. During the second period, Espen Knutsen fired an errant shot that flew into the stands, bounced off of a spectator, and hit Brittanie in the temple. Forty-eight hours later she was dead, just one day before her fourteenth birthday.

The simple truth is that all of life is a risk. If you walk across a street, take a boat ride, fly in an airplane, invest your money, swallow a pill, ride in a car, eat in a restaurant, or go to a hockey game, you are taking a risk.

A few years ago I was asked to do a workshop at the Florida Christian Convention in Jacksonville. That morning, while stepping out of the shower, I slipped and fell flat on my back on the hard tile floor. The crash brought Marilyn running to see what was wrong. She found me in a pool of water, in excruciating pain. I honestly thought I had broken my back. It took me several minutes to get to my feet, and even then I couldn't twist or bend. I eventually did make it to my workshop, but I was walking like Frankenstein the whole day and taking aspirin to deaden the pain. Naturally, I made it a point never to take a shower again as long as I lived.

Just kidding.

Of course I didn't swear off showers. I understand that what happened to me was just one of those crazy things that happen in the normal routine of a person's life. It doesn't matter how careful you are, accidents happen. There are certain unavoidable risks in life.

Second, there are NECESSARY RISKS. As I'm writing these words, American soldiers are fighting Al-Qaeda forces in the mountains of Afghanistan. A few days ago, a Navy SEAL, Petty officer Neil Roberts, fell from a Chinook helicopter when it came under heavy fire. His comrades managed to escape, though the chopper was speckled with bullet holes. They didn't stay away for long, however, because American soldiers live and operate according to a steadfast code of honor: They never abandon their dead and wounded on the battlefield.

The reconnaissance team, let by Sgt. John Chapman, made its escape, regrouped, and then turned right around and flew back into harm's way. Once again, the chopper came under heavy fire, and this time crash landed. John Chapman was the first man out, followed by twenty-one of our finest Special Ops forces. Chapman sprayed gunfire over enemy positions as his men dispersed and tried to find cover. In doing so, he was protecting his men, but exposing himself to the enemy. Several bullets slammed into his chest.

Our soldiers wound up fighting the rest of the day to keep the enemy at bay, knowing they had no hope of being rescued until nightfall. Finally, under the cover of darkness, a rescue chopper picked up the men from the combat zone and returned to base. There, seven dead Americans were unloaded, including the body of Petty Officer Roberts.

Those men were taking a huge risk when they flew back into the line of fire, but it was a necessary risk. The military thrives on a "band of brothers" mentality that places value on every soldier, from the decorated commander to the raw recruit. Whether storming a beachhead or flushing terrorists out of a cave, every soldier needs to know that his team will support him to the bitter end. Without that assurance, very few men or women would be willing to lay their lives on the line.

You may not be in the military, but you, too, will face some necessary risks during your lifetime. In 2001 my father was diagnosed with rectal cancer, which is one of the deadliest forms of cancer in men. His doctor looked him square in the eye and said, "You're going to need chemo, radiation, and surgery or you'll die." That sounds simple enough. After all, people have cancer surgery and treatments every day and live to tell about it. But Dad's case was different. He had a multitude of other problems, including a bad heart and diabetes. The surgery was going to be extremely high-risk. But with the only other option being certain death, it was a necessary risk.

Sometimes life leaves us with only one viable option. It can be frightening and dangerous, but the only choice we have is to plow ahead.

Third, there are CALCULATED RISKS. A calculated risk differs from a necessary risk in that there is at least a second or third option that could be taken. During the Spanish-American War, a group of army doctors was studying yellow fever. Specifically, they were trying to find out how it was passed from one person to another. They suspected that mosquitoes were the culprits and set out to prove it. Their first step was to allow some mosquitoes to feed on yellow-fever patients and then let them bite some guinea pigs. When the guinea pigs became infected, it proved that mosquitoes could give yellow fever to animals, but it didn't necessarily prove that they could give it to people.

So the next logical step was to run the experiment again using people instead of guinea pigs.

But that's where they ran into a problem.

Whom could they ask to participate in such an experiment? Who in his right mind would want to expose himself to such a dangerous and deadly disease? Finally, the doctors decided to try the experiment on themselves. They allowed some infected mosquitoes to crawl all over their bodies and chew on them as much as they wanted. And sure enough. They got the fever.

Then there was one final question they had to answer: Could a person get yellow fever simply by being around someone who had it?

Again some doctors moved into a house that was inhabited by a number of yellow-fever patients. They wore their clothes, slept in their beds, and shared facilities. When not one of those doctors became infected with the disease, it was apparent that the fever couldn't be passed around simply through close contact between people.

So were those doctors foolish?

No, they were brave, committed men who were willing to risk their lives for the greater good of mankind. They knew that what they were doing was dangerous, and they could have declined. No one would have blamed them. But they also knew it was important. They knew they might unlock a mystery that would save countless lives. So they weighed the dangers against the potential rewards and determined that the experiment was a risk worth taking.

No doubt you've done the same thing.

You probably did it when you got married. You knew that marriage is risky business. You knew that even people who start out head-over-heels in love sometimes end up in divorce court. But you weighed the dangers alongside the potential rewards and decided it was a risk worth taking.

Or maybe you did it when you changed jobs.

Back in 1989 I had my choice of two jobs. Both were ministry related, but one offered good money and the other offered considerably less than I was already making. One offered stability and the other offered uncertainty. One offered a full support staff and the other offered an electric typewriter and a desk lamp with a burnt-out light bulb. On the surface, it was a no-brainer. But the longer Marilyn and I talked and the closer we looked at the lesser of the two opportunities, the more we were drawn to it. We made lists of pros and cons and weighed every conceivable factor. We sought counsel and prayed like mad. Finally, we just decided to go for it.

In November 1989 I accepted the call to be the preacher and the only staff member of a small group of believers in Kissimmee, Florida. They called themselves Poinciana Christian Church. They had a tiny little building on a dead-end street and no money. (Not exactly the kind of situation most preachers are looking for!) Yet there was a spirit about them that was undeniably upbeat. I sensed a lot of love and a sincere faith. They told me that they wanted to grow and that they weren't afraid of change. Yes, it was a risky move. But it was all carefully calculated. I went in with my eyes open. I thought through every possibility and I was willing to accept whatever happened.

Now Poinciana Christian Church is a true force for God in one of the fastest-growing counties in America. We're not on a dead-end street anymore, I'm no longer using an old dilapidated typewriter, and we can actually afford light bulbs. I have a support staff that is second to none and the privilege of preaching every week to people who treat my family and me with love and respect.

Life is good.

That's not to say it wouldn't have been good if I'd taken the other job. But in my mind the experience proves that it's wise not to make decisions too quickly. Sometimes we have a tendency to grab the easy, obvious choice without thoroughly considering the lesser alternatives. I've learned that it's the carefully calculated risk that often brings the biggest rewards.

> IT'S WISE NOT TO MAKE DECISIONS TOO QUICKLY. SOMETIMES WE HAVE A TENDENCY TO GRAB THE EASY, OBVIOUS CHOICE WITHOUT THOROUGHLY CONSIDERING THE LESSER ALTERNATIVES.

Fourth, there are FOOLISH RISKS. MSNBC.com carried a story about the residents of an apartment complex in Delaware who reported a foul smell coming from a unit where a forty-five-year-old man lived alone. No one had seen the man for several days and wondered if something terrible had happened. When police entered the apartment, they found that something terrible had indeed happened. Something more terrible than any of them could have imagined. The man was dead in the middle of the floor and was surrounded by eight rattlesnakes and two cobras. The door to a nearby cage was open, leading to speculation that the man had forgotten to close it or hadn't fastened it properly.

What makes a man bring a cobra home instead of a puppy dog?

I suppose the same thing that makes him drive eighty-five in a fifty-five mile-an-hour zone.

Or continue playing golf with lightning crackling on the horizon.

Or flirt with a woman who is not his wife.

Or cheat on his income tax.

Or smoke cigarettes.

Or use drugs.

It's easy to assume that foolish risks are simply the result of stupidity, but in the case of strong men, I believe it's often more of a testosterone issue. Like Samson, strong men often do crazy things because they believe they're invincible. They think they can do whatever they want and nothing will happen. Why? Because nothing ever *has* happened. It's a simple fact that with every sinful indulgence that produces no harmful result, we grow more comfortable and complacent, eventually coming to believe that the activity is not really dangerous at all.

In the case of Samson, we know he sinned with three different women, but no one believes that was the extent of his philandering. In fact, by the time we reach Judges 16, it appears that he was no longer interested in marriage, but, rather, was only seeking sex. The parade of women through his life would probably astonish us if we knew the whole story. We know he had some close calls, as in the case of his visit to the prostitute in Gaza, but with each successful tryst, Samson's guard dropped lower and lower.

> WITH EVERY SINFUL INDULGENCE THAT PRODUCES NO HARMFUL RESULT, WE GROW MORE COMFORTABLE AND COMPLACENT, EVENTUALLY COMING TO BELIEVE THAT THE ACTIVITY IS NOT REALLY DANGEROUS AT ALL.

And then a woman named Delilah entered the picture.

Here's something to remember: A foolish risk is still a foolish risk, even if you don't get caught. It could even be true that *not* getting caught is the worst thing that could happen to you, for it almost guarantees that you'll indulge again.

A FOOLISH RISK IS STILL A FOOLISH RISK, EVEN IF YOU DON'T GET CAUGHT.

Let me stress again that risk taking can be a very good thing. Will Rogers once said, "Why shouldn't I go out on a limb? Isn't that where the fruit is?" Necessary risks and calculated risks can bring some sweet fruit into our lives. But foolish risks will only bring us trouble and despair.

SIX QUESTIONS THAT COULD SAVE YOUR LIFE

Let me offer you a system that will help you avoid foolish risks. I believe there are six simple questions you can ask that, if answered honestly, will keep you from ruining your life with some frivolous or irrational act.

Question #1: Are the rewards worth as much as the consequences might cost me? The "running of the bulls" is the most famous event of the Fiesta of San Fermin in Pamplona, Spain. The idea is to move the bulls from their pen to the bullring, a distance of a half mile. A fence is constructed along the street from the pen to the ring and people are invited to provide incentive for the bulls to make the run. Every morning for a week they gather in front of the pen where the bulls are kept. At 8:00 A.M., a rocket is fired and the bulls are let loose. As the bulls come charging into the street, the people begin running for their lives. Since no man can outrun a bull, the key to survival is to avoid the bulls by ducking through cracks in the fence, leaping over the fence, or finding a cleft to press into.

In 1995 two young Americans were visiting Pamplona with a friend. They got caught up in the spirit of the festival and decided to take part in the bull running. They figured it would provide an incredible adrenaline rush and give them a good story to tell to their friends back home. The problem was, one of the young men slipped and fell during the running. As he struggled to get to his feet, an enormous bull impaled him on his massive horns. He was pronounced dead at a nearby hospital a few minutes later.

Think about the greatest potential consequence of their choice. It was sudden, violent death. Now think about the greatest potential reward. It was a brief adrenaline rush and a good story to tell to their friends.

Does that sound like a good trade to you?

Yet strong men make similar trades every day.

Take the man who allows himself to be drawn into a romantic relationship with a coworker. He sneaks a kiss in the office or a phone call after hours or a rendezvous at a restaurant in another town. And all while his wife is at home with their two kids. The man has no intention of leaving his wife; he's just out to have a little fun. But is the fun he's having worth the risk of destroying his family and his reputation?

My friend, in every risk scenario there will be potential consequences and potential rewards. The key to making good decisions is to weigh them very carefully. If what you could lose exceeds what you stand to gain, then it's a choice you need to turn and run away from. Ask yourself if you'd be willing to live with the potential consequences of the act for the rest of your life.

Question #2: Have I fully researched the risk? In the late 1990s, "day-trading" became very popular among investors in the stock market. With a home computer and an Internet connection you could buy and sell stocks all day long from the comfort of your living room. And because many tech stocks were ridiculously overvalued and producing huge prices, millions of people were jumping into the market who knew nothing about it. I know people who bought stocks without even knowing what the company they were investing in produced! Needless to say, many people lost a lot of money when the economy went sour.

> "DON'T EVER TEST THE DEPTH OF A RIVER WITH BOTH FEET."

There's an old Indian proverb that says, "Don't ever test the depth of a river with both feet." That's good advice. Don't ever jump feetfirst into a business deal, a job, a relationship, or any other life-altering arrangement unless you've done your homework. Proverbs 2:3–4 says, "Cry out for insight and understanding. Search for them as you would for lost money or hidden treasure."

Question #3: What has happened to other people who have taken the same risk? Solomon said, "History merely repeats itself. It has all been done before" (Eccles. 1:9). That means you can help yourself make good decisions simply by becoming a student of history.

During the height of the Bill Clinton/Monica Lewinsky sex scandal, I spoke to a strong, successful man who'd just ended an illicit sexual affair. He said that the nightly news reports began to haunt him. As the evidence against Mr. Clinton mounted and his shame and embarrassment grew, the man began to picture the same thing happening to him. He said that if the president of the United States, with all his resources, couldn't hide his cheating, he knew he'd never be able to either. So he broke off the illicit relationship and recommitted himself to his wife.

Now, I know what you're thinking. You're thinking that the fear of getting caught is not a very noble motivation for ending the affair. And you're right. But without a doubt it's better than nothing. In fact, the Bible encourages us to be afraid of exposure. Numbers 32:23 says, "You may be sure that your sin will find you out." And the story of Achan and the story of David's affair with Bathsheba seem specifically designed to help us realize the ultimate futility of hiding sin.

If you are involved in some risky, questionable behavior right now, or if you're feeling inclined to indulge, I urge you to become a student of history. Take note of what has happened to other men who have chosen the same road. If you see a string of disastrous results and broken lives, please don't be foolish enough to think your situation will end differently. Recognize the warning for what it is and correct your behavior.

Question #4: What is my motivation for taking this risk? My favorite risk story in the Bible is found in 2 Samuel 23. David and his men were hiding in the cave of Adullam and were surrounded by Philistines. The conditions were harsh and David and his men were hungry and thirsty. In a moment of longing, David remarked that he'd love to have a drink of water from the well that sat near the entrance to the village of Bethlehem. We know it was an off-hand comment, the kind you make when you're dreaming out loud, because Bethlehem was being occupied by a detachment of Philistine soldiers. David fully understood that the well was inaccessible at the moment.

But three of David's elite soldiers overheard the comment and retreated to a dark corner of the cave to put their heads together. They loved David and knew that he'd been under incredible stress. They knew that even more than being physically refreshed by the drink of water, he would be encouraged by the devotion of three men who were willing to risk their lives to give it to him. And so, without telling David, they crept out of the cave under the cover of darkness, worked their way through enemy lines, drew a container of water from the well, and returned to the cave.

There's something indescribably beautiful about that story. One could easily make the case that the three men were foolish to risk life and limb simply for a drink of water. Yet there's so much love in their actions that we simply can't think negatively toward them. I'm certainly not suggesting that the right motivation makes any risk worth taking. Jumping off of a ten-story building is a bad idea, even if you are doing it to show your wife how much you love her. However, in a "me-first" world like ours, a noble, selfless motive is refreshing and would always make a borderline risk seem more worth taking.

Question #5: What will my life be like if I don't take this risk? In 1996, the renowned mountain climber, Rob Hall, was leading an expedition to the top of Mt. Everest. In the expedition were a variety of people who were not experienced climbers, but were wealthy enough to afford the sixty-thousand-dollar fee that Hall's company charged for trips to the top of the world's tallest mountain. The expedition began uneventfully, but before the team had time to reach the summit and return to camp, a massive storm swept through the Himalayas. Temperatures dropped to -140 degrees Fahrenheit, and screaming winds blew snow horizontally with such force that the flakes felt like bee stings. One member of the expedition later said the "whiteout" was so extreme it was like being trapped in a bottle of milk.

Doug Hansen, a novice climber and postal worker from Kent, Washington, quickly began suffering from the effects of frostbite and extreme fatigue. When it became apparent that he would not be able to make it back to camp, Rob Hall had a decision to make: He could either return to camp and save himself, leaving Hansen to die, or he could stay with his client until the storm passed and risk losing his own life.

Rob Hall's logic was simple. His contract with his clients promised that he would take them both up *and down* the mountain. It guaranteed that he would be with them every step of the way. Thus, he believed that if he left his client behind to save his own neck, he would justifiably be branded a liar and a coward and would lose not only the respect of the climbing fraternity, but his own self-respect. So Rob Hall decided to stay with Mr. Hansen. Their frozen bodies were recovered the next day, half buried in the snow.

IT'S OFTEN TRUE THAT NOT TAKING A RISK IS A BIGGER RISK THAN TAKING IT.

You may never find yourself in a whiteout on Mt. Everest, but there's a very good chance that you'll someday find yourself in a situation similar to the one Rob Hall was in. Sometimes we refer to it as being "between a rock and a hard place." It's that moment when you realize that there's danger in both directions, that no matter which way you turn, something bad is probably going to happen. When you come to that place, you must determine the more noble choice, even if it carries the greatest risk to your physical well-being, and go for it. It's often true that *not* taking a risk is a bigger risk than taking it.

Question #6: What does the Bible say about what I am thinking about doing? Not long ago I was watching a war movie on television. A group of soldiers was walking casually across an open field when one of them suddenly spotted a land mine. At the top of his lungs, he screamed, "Mines!" and the soldiers all froze in their tracks. No one dared move a muscle. All casual conversations came to a halt, and cold sweat broke out on their faces.

It was a scary scene that made me think. In a sense, life is a mine field. Satan sets subtle, almost invisible traps for us everywhere. That's why we need the Word of God. David said, "Your word is a lamp for my feet and a light for my path" (Ps. 119:105). In other words, it shows us where the mines are. It keeps us from making that one fatal step or taking that one foolish risk that could ruin our lives.

Unfortunately, strong men sometimes fail to give the Word of God the attention it deserves. Like Samson, they tend to rely on their own strength and cunning. But in that old war movie I was watching, it was one of the strongest, most confident soldiers in the platoon that got his leg blown off. It doesn't matter how strong or clever you are, you need a lamp for your feet and a light for your path.

Right now a car company is running a series of ads that says, "If you're not living on the edge, you're taking up too much room." I don't know anything about the car business, but I think that slogan would be a good one for the church. We Christians come from a long line of risk takers; from Abraham, who packed up everything he owned and set out for an unknown land, to Rahab, who risked her life to hide some enemy spies, to Peter, who stepped out of a boat and walked on water. I believe God wants His people to be bold and forward thinking, to live on the edge.

My only plea is that we not be foolish. Before you take any risk: Make sure the rewards outweigh the potential consequences. Make sure you've done your homework.

Make sure you know what's happened to others who've taken the same risk.

Make sure your motivation is pure.

Make sure you've looked at all your options.

And make sure you've consulted God's Word.

TEN

STRONG MEN TEND TO STRUGGLE WITH INTIMACY

Marriage starts the moment a man and woman become one. The trouble starts the moment they start trying to decide which one.

—GEORGE BURNS

As the Scriptures say, "A man leaves his father and mother and is joined to his wife, and the two are united into one."

—PAUL THE APOSTLE (EPHESIANS 5:31)

THE MOST FAMOUS PART OF SAMSON'S STORY CONCERNS his disastrous affair with Delilah, a conniving young woman from the valley of Sorek. Many scholars believe she was half Samson's age, probably about twenty, and drop-dead gorgeous. We're not told how or where they met, though knowing Samson, I wouldn't be surprised if he simply spotted her walking down the street and began pursuing her, not letting up until she gave in to his overtures. The Bible says he fell in love with her, so we can't exactly say that he viewed her merely as a plaything. Yet, considering Samson's track record with the opposite sex, it's hard to imagine his "love" extending very far beyond the spike in blood pressure he felt when he ran his eyes over the curve of her hip.

Though twenty years have now passed since he first set his sights on the girl from Timnah, we can see that Samson hasn't learned much about love and romance. In fact, even a casual comparison of the two relationships reveals a striking similarity. Both with the girl from Timnah and Delilah, Samson was aloof and standoffish. He refused to share his innermost secrets and feelings. He forced both women to beg him for information. In short, he resisted intimacy.

Of course, you could say that Samson's reticence was nothing more than caution. You could say that he was simply being careful because he was suspicious of their motives. But that would seem to be giving him more credit than he deserves. Nothing in either passage suggests that Samson suspected his women were plotting to betray him. In fact, in the case of Delilah, his willingness to share his deepest secret virtually proves that he trusted her completely. No, Samson's problem was simply that he struggled with intimacy. And so do a lot of other strong men.

As I was discussing this book with a female friend, she made the following observation: "Any woman who picks up this book and scans the table of contents will turn to the chapter on intimacy first. That's the one thing that most married women are starved for." I think she's right. I've been counseling married couples for over a quarter of a century, and this is the problem I see over and over, even among Christians. There are too many walls and secrets in our marriages. We're sharing beds, but not feelings. Our schedules are full, but our hearts are empty. One young mother described it this way: "My husband and I don't have a marriage, we have a business. We make money, pay bills, and raise kids, period."

Of course, any marriage can lack intimacy, but I believe that a strong man's marriage will be more likely than most to suffer in this area. Consider the following factors that a woman almost always has to contend with in her strong-man husband.

Busyness. Strong men are almost always busy men. They hold positions of responsibility and are often called upon to work long hours. They are also likely to have numerous hobbies and recreational interests outside of their work.

Ambition. Many strong men have goals that extend far beyond their families. They seek the kind of power and status that can only be achieved by competing head-to-head with other strong, talented men. Often, their focus is more on their competitors than on their wives.

Impatience. Strong men who are in positions of authority are often used to getting what they want whenever they want it. Things happen quickly around them because when they speak, people jump. But intimacy takes time to build and must be done slowly. A strong man is likely to find the process very frustrating.

> STRONG, SUCCESSFUL MEN WHO KNOW THEY ARE NEGLECTING THEIR WIVES OFTEN TRY TO MAKE UP FOR IT BY SHOWERING THEM WITH GIFTS. THEY MISTAKENLY BELIEVE THAT MATERIAL THINGS CAN MAKE UP FOR A LACK OF TIME AND ATTENTION.

Distraction. Because strong men carry a lot of responsibility, they naturally have a lot on their minds. Even if they want to, it's difficult for them to leave their work at the office. One woman recently told me that her husband typically receives three or four phone calls from his office every evening. And when they're out together, she says her husband talks to his cell phone more than he talks to her.

Money. Strong, successful men who know they are neglecting their wives often try to make up for it by showering them with gifts. They mistakenly believe that material things can make up for a lack of time and attention.

Attraction (to and by the opposite sex). Strong men always attract women and can easily be attracted to them. No one knows this better than a wife who's sitting at home wondering why her husband is working so late . . . again.

Fatigue. Even strong men get tired. After a man has worked hard and borne a lot of pressure all day, he can easily feel he has nothing left to give to his wife when he gets home.

As I reflect on these factors, I'm reminded of a television interview I saw a few years ago. A woman who had once been married to an internationally famous entertainer was talking about her current marriage to a man who made ten dollars an hour. When asked what the primary difference was between the two men, she said, "My current husband knows I'm alive."

Strong man, have you checked lately to see if your wife is still alive?

How long has it been since you had a heart-to-heart talk with her?

How long has it been since you asked her if anything was bothering her?

How long has it been since you spent an entire day alone with her?

How long has it been since you cried together?

How long has it been since you shared a secret with her?

How long has it been since you wrote her a love letter?

How long has it been since you gave her a backrub?

How long has it been since you surprised her with a weekend getaway?

How long has it been since you sat together in a room with a television without turning it on?

How long has it been since you got so wrapped up in a conversation with her that you lost all track of time?

How long has it been since your lovemaking lasted for more than fifteen minutes?

How long has it been since you made love without rolling over afterward and falling asleep?

If these questions feel like pin pricks in your conscience, then it's safe to say the Samson Syndrome has you in its grip and that you're in need of an intimacy makeover.

THE RIGHT PERSPECTIVE

The first step in the pursuit of intimacy in marriage is to develop the proper state of mind. If intimacy hasn't been a priority for you in the past, then your whole concept of your marriage and your role in it has to change. Here are three facts you need to catch hold of.

First, it takes TWO to build intimacy. There are a lot of duties in marriage that can be handled by either the husband or the wife. Laundry, yard work, cooking, cleaning, car maintenance, bill paying, and a host of other duties can be divided up according to the couple's talents and interests. Working as a team during the early years, most couples will try different combinations until they find a system that works. But when it comes to intimacy, *both* the husband and the wife have to be totally involved and committed. In fact, I think the case can be made that the husband is primarily responsible for creating an environment where intimacy can flourish.

I say that because the Bible commands husbands to love their wives, but never commands wives to love their husbands. It's true. Ephesians 5:25 says, "You husbands must love your wives with the same love Christ showed the church." But nowhere can you find the same command directed toward wives. Seems unfair, doesn't it?

ROMANTIC LOVE IS, BY NATURE, RECIPROCAL. THAT IS, IT GROWS THROUGH A SERIES OF OVERTURES AND RESPONSES.

But it isn't, and here's why.

Romantic love is, by nature, reciprocal. That is, it grows through a series of overtures and responses. For example, when two people first meet, they don't just instantly decide to pursue a romantic relationship. Even if there's a strong physical attraction, nothing is going to develop unless one person or the other makes an overture. That overture will then produce either a positive or a negative response. If the response is negative, chances are the two people will go their separate ways like the proverbial ships passing in the night. But if the response is positive, then another overture will certainly be forthcoming. And then another response . . . and another overture . . . and another response . . . until the relationship is either off and running or dead in the water.

In Ephesians 5, Paul is simply saying that the husband should be proactive in loving his wife. He should be actively creating an environment where their love can flourish. Long after the vows have been exchanged, he should still be making overtures that create positive responses from her. Of course, this is not to say that the wife can never make an overture of her own. Indeed, she can. (And if she's smart, she will!) But God intends for the husband to take the lead and be proactive.

Friend, are you doing your part to create love and intimacy in your marriage? When was the last time you went out of your way to do something thoughtful and sweet and totally unexpected for your wife? I asked this question of some of my friends and several of them had to wrinkle up their noses and rack their brains to try to remember. Let me give you a clue: If it's been longer than twenty-four to forty-eight hours, then it's been too long. You probably need to put this book down and get busy!

Second, it takes TIME to build intimacy. My wife, Marilyn, and I have been married since 1975. We were high-school sweethearts and dated for four years before we got married between my sophomore and junior years in Bible college. Our marriage has always been good, but in recent years it's reached a level of intimacy that often amazes me. For example, Marilyn knows what I'm going to say before I say it. Sometimes, when I'm shaping my lips to speak, she'll blurt the words out ahead of me. Then she smiles in that way that only a wife can and says, "I can read you like a book." Of course, my male ego compels me to argue with her on that point, but deep down we both know it's true.

Also, we've reached the point at which we can communicate without words. On numerous occasions we've merely glanced at each other and burst out laughing. We have a million little private jokes that no one else in the world would understand, and when something happens that triggers the thought of one, we can just look at each other and start giggling. Sometimes when we're out with friends, they'll look at us with confused expressions and say, "What's so funny?"

A lot of people equate intimacy with sex. In fact, we often refer to having sex as "being intimate." But true intimacy extends far beyond the physical. True intimacy comes when you've peeled away all the layers of another person's nature and gained access to his or her soul. It's knowing the other person's thoughts, sharing the other person's feelings, and understanding the other person's needs. It's a level of familiarity that can only come through years of hard work and shared experiences.

TRUE INTIMACY COMES WHEN YOU'VE PEELED AWAY ALL THE LAYERS OF ANOTHER PERSON'S NATURE AND GAINED ACCESS TO HIS OR HER SOUL.

Third, it takes TROUBLE to build intimacy. Nobody wants to go through hard times. I don't know a single person who relishes trouble. But the truth is that trouble, perhaps more than anything else, brings people together. When storm clouds roll in, husbands and wives are forced to unite and often discover hidden strengths and noble qualities in each other that were never apparent when the sun was shining.

A woman named Jackie was diagnosed with terminal cancer at the age of forty-two. Both she and her husband were career-minded people who led busy lives. They shared a home, but not much else. Their paths crossed in bed every night and they found the time to go out to dinner occasionally, but for the most part they moved in different circles, had different friends, and were pursuing different goals.

But Jackie's illness forced them to slam on the brakes and reevaluate. The knowledge that her days were numbered suddenly made their career pursuits seem trivial. Jackie's husband impulsively decided to quit his job so he could be with her for the rest of her days on earth. For the next eighteen months they were together every day. Before she died, Jackie said that she had never really known her husband. They had run a household and made love on a regular basis for several years, but it wasn't until she got sick that she began to discover the true depths of his character.

Often, you'll hear couples who've been through hard times say, "This situation has brought us closer together." I'm not suggesting that you should start praying for trouble in the hope that it will be a tonic for your marriage, but I do believe that when trouble comes, it will bring with it an opportunity to deepen your relationship.

THE RIGHT PLAN

Once you've gained the right perspective on intimacy, it's important to start applying it to your daily life. Based on my experience and my observations of others, there are several positive steps you can take.

First, make it a point to spend quality time with your wife. The key word here is *quality,* as Marilyn and I have discovered. We are in a unique situation in that she is my secretary. She is the last person I see when I leave the house in the morning, the first person I see when I get to the office, the last person I see when I leave the office, and the first person I see when I get home at the end of the day. Unless I'm traveling, we are literally together all day every day. Nobody can say I don't spend time with my wife!

But not all of it is *quality* time.

At the office I am often behind a closed door writing a sermon, counseling someone, or talking on the phone. At the same time, she is juggling a hundred responsibilities that I don't even pretend to know anything about. We talk, but it's usually about business. The phone rings off the hook, people stop by to chat, and occasional brush fires break out that we have to deal with on the spur of the moment. When we get home at the end of the day, we're both exhausted. The honest truth is that we can spend an entire work week together and feel as though we haven't done anything to enhance our relationship.

So we made a deal.

We decided that Saturday would be *our* day. The church can have us Sunday through Friday. I'll talk to my agent and my editor and anyone else who needs a piece of me on those days. But when Saturday comes, it's Mark-and-Marilyn time. I don't play golf with the guys and Marilyn doesn't go shopping with the girls. We spend the whole day together doing nothing but fun stuff. Sometimes we leave the house early and have an all-day adventure. We might go to the beach, to Disney, to the mall, to a movie, or to a flea market. Or we might just stay home and lounge around all day. Sometimes we play our favorite CDs for hours or watch an old movie. Of course, I'm available to my people when emergencies arise, but I do everything I can to keep the world from infringing on our quality time.

And let me tell you, our little arrangement has paid tremendous dividends. It gives us a time of refreshing to look forward to every week. It provides opportunities for us to talk about things that have nothing to do with our work. And it takes us to places where we can laugh and have fun together.

I know that some couples might find such an arrangement hard to accomplish. You, for example, may have young children that can't be left alone. Or your work schedule may not allow you and your wife to spend a whole day together. However, you must spend at least *some* quality time together on a regular basis if you want to achieve intimacy in your relationship. All work and no play makes for a dull marriage!

Second, give your wife the gift of words. In my opinion, a huge deception has been perpetrated on the human race. Somebody managed to convince us that women are talkers and men aren't. Yes, I've heard the old line that a woman speaks sixty-thousand words a day and a man speaks twenty-five-thousand. Personally, I'd like to know who figured that out and how. I'm no behavioral scientist, but I can tell you that when I'm with a group of men, the chatter never stops! Put four guys in a golf foursome and just try to get a word in edgewise! Or load some guys in a car and send them to a baseball game. They'll all blow past the twenty-five-thousand word mark before the seventh-inning stretch!

Face it, words are not the problem.

Subject matter is the problem.

I remember seeing a Dilbert cartoon that showed a man talking to a woman. The woman says, "I like men who know how to communicate, but not a man who only talks about sports, computers, his job, TV, sex, or his accomplishments." Puzzled, the man says, "That only leaves Greek mythology and you to talk about." And the woman says, "I hate Greek mythology."

I've found that a lot of husbands feel like the poor soul in that cartoon. They think their wives aren't interested in the things they're interested in. That may be true in a few cases, but not generally. I've been counseling couples for over twenty-five years, and I have *never* heard a wife say that she didn't care about the things that were important to her husband. One woman recently said to me, "I would be happy for my husband to talk about *anything!*"

Friend, talk to your wife.

Take her for a walk. Hold her hand and ask her about her day. Then tell her about yours.

Or take her to a nice restaurant she's been wanting to try. But don't just wolf down your food and ask for the check. Sit there for a while. Dine. Have an extra cup of coffee and let your dinner settle. Then order the most outrageous dessert on the menu and ask for two spoons. Savor it. And savor the moment. Look into her eyes and remember all the reasons you fell in love with her in the first place. Tell her you love her and just ride the conversation to wherever it wants to go. I promise it'll take you to a wonderful place.

> IF YOU REALLY WANT TO BLOW HER MIND, CRAWL INTO BED SOME NIGHT AND DON'T REACH FOR THE REMOTE.

Or, if you really want to blow her mind, crawl into bed some night and don't reach for the remote, don't roll over and start snoring, and don't start making sexual advances. Instead, prop yourself up on your elbow, offer to rub her back, and start reminiscing about some pleasant experience the two of you once shared. But be prepared. You could be in for a very long (and wonderful) night!

Give your wife the gift of words.

Third, protect the dignity and privacy of your marriage. The heart of intimacy is found in the private things a husband and wife share that are precious and personal and nobody else's business. A while back I attended a wedding ceremony where the groom turned the traditional kiss into a honeymoon sneak preview. He took what should have been a tender expression of love and cheapened it. He dragged it out to an inappropriate length and added enough theatrics and body language to draw hoots and hollers from the congregation. When he finally tore his mouth off of his bride's with a loud smack, he wore the smirk of a guy who had just pulled a fast one. I actually thought he was going to pump his fist in the air and high-five his best man. Sadly, his new wife looked thoroughly surprised and embarrassed.

I could be wrong (and I hope I am), but I have a bad feeling about their marriage. If the man intentionally embarrassed his wife in front of a crowd of people on their wedding day and thought nothing of it, how many more times will he embarrass her over the years? And at what point will her embarrassment turn to resentment? I've known men before who seemed not to understand that there are just some things in marriage that should be kept behind closed doors. And not surprisingly, those guys always seem to have lousy marriages.

Solomon said, "There is a time for everything . . . a time to be quiet and a time to speak up" (Eccles. 3:1a, 7b). Let me challenge you to be quiet about the things you and your wife share that are nobody else's business. Details regarding your sex life, your finances, or your private conversations shouldn't be hung out like underwear on a clothesline for everyone to see. Keeping those things to yourself proves that you respect your mate and that you value those things that make your relationship unique. It will also encourage an even deeper level of intimacy because your wife will know she can trust you. She'll never be afraid to allow you to enter the deepest chambers of her heart.

> DETAILS REGARDING YOUR SEX LIFE, YOUR FINANCES, OR YOUR PRIVATE CONVERSATIONS SHOULDN'T BE HUNG OUT LIKE UNDERWEAR ON A CLOTHESLINE FOR EVERYONE TO SEE.

Fourth, make your wife your primary source of emotional support. We all need to talk about the things that are important to us or that we're struggling with. We need someone who will listen and sympathize or offer encouragement and advice. Many women desperately want to be that person for their husbands, but find that their husbands look elsewhere for someone to meet that need.

I'm convinced this is one reason why so many strong men have affairs with their secretaries and coworkers. It's not a matter of wanting or even needing sex. More often, it's a matter of establishing an intimate bond with someone you're sharing your deepest feelings with and who is providing emotional support and encouragement.

I remember talking to a man who was deeply embroiled in an affair with a coworker. He admitted that the illicit feelings started shortly after they began talking regularly on their breaks and at lunch. He said there was never any sexual talk, just a lot of blowing off steam and mutual sympathizing. On one particular day when he was especially upset, she reached out and took his hand. He said the touch of her skin was electric and from that moment on, nothing was ever quite the same. I asked him why he didn't allow his wife to be his primary source of emotional support, and he gave a truly lame answer. He said, "My wife is at home while I'm at work. She's never there when I need her." The truth is that it's not always convenient to make your wife your primary source of emotional support. You need to do it anyway.

Is there an attractive woman at your workplace that you've grown especially fond of talking to? Could it be that you're developing a relationship that, while not crossing the line of inappropriate behavior, is still weaving an emotional bond that is getting stronger and stronger? Sure, you tell yourself it's all innocent and that nothing is going to happen. And you might be right. But keep in mind that virtually every man who's ever been ruined by an office affair said the same thing.

If you're in this situation, I plead with you to cut the bond. You can do it without being rude or unkind. Just be truthful and firm, and then turn back to the person God gave you. Let your wife be your sounding board, your counselor, your encourager. Don't be concerned that she doesn't have a grasp on issues. She may not work in your office or understand every aspect of your business, but she knows *you*, probably better than anyone else, and that makes her uniquely qualified to be your primary source of emotional support. And what's more, she *wants* to fill that role. She *needs* to hold that place in your life.

If you want to start cultivating intimacy in your marriage . . .

Make it a point to spend quality time with your wife.

Give her the gift of words.

Protect the dignity and privacy of your marriage.

And let her be your primary source of emotional support.

ELEVEN

STRONG MEN TEND TO TAKE TOO MUCH FOR GRANTED

FIRST MAN: "Do you take your wife for granted?"
SECOND MAN: "Not anymore."
FIRST MAN: "What happened?"
SECOND MAN: "A month after we moved from New York to Kansas City I noticed that we still had the same mailman."
—CLASSIC COMEDY ROUTINE

What makes us think we can escape if we are indifferent . . . ?
—HEBREWS 2:3

AS I SIT DOWN TO WRITE THIS CHAPTER, IT'S A HOLIDAY. The calendar doesn't designate it as such, but for me and millions of golf lovers worldwide, it is. You see, today is the day they play the opening round of the Masters. The Masters is the most storied event in golf, and perhaps in all of sports. Forget the trophies, the million-dollar paychecks, and the lucrative endorsement contracts. Every professional golfer's ultimate dream is to win a green jacket. It's easily golf's greatest honor, the ultimate career maker.

Like any great sporting event, the Masters has produced

moments of incredible drama. A few players have experienced their finest moments in those hallowed north-Georgia hills, and many their worst. And then there are those, like Arnold Palmer, who have experienced both. As the owner of four green jackets, Arnie has enjoyed some of his greatest days at Augusta National. But there is one day I'm sure he'd like to forget.

The year was 1961. After four days of battling the greatest course and the greatest players in the world, Arnie came to the final hole needing only a par to win. He stepped up on the tee and launched a powerful drive that settled in the middle of the fairway. As the crowd cheered and the folks in Butler Cabin searched the racks to find a jacket in his size, Arnie did something unusual and very out of character. He stopped to accept a congratulatory handshake from an old friend. The man's name was George Low. He was a noted golf-club designer and had designed the putter Arnie was using.

Rarely does a great champion celebrate a victory before it's won, and when he does, bad things almost always happen. Such was the case with Arnie. With his concentration broken, he pushed his second shot, causing it to land in the right-hand bunker. Then he clipped too much of the ball on his sand shot and blasted it over the green. From there he chipped back onto the green and missed his bogey putt. His tap-in for six left the crowd stunned and gave Gary Player the championship.

Clearly, Arnie took too much for granted. He should have stayed focused on the job at hand and saved the congratulatory handshakes for after the tournament. On the other hand, it's easy to see how such a thing could happen. Arnie was the Tiger Woods of that era. He'd already won two green jackets (in 1958 and 1960) and was the most feared competitor on the tour. His gallery, nicknamed "Arnie's Army," answered his every move with a deafening roar of approval, and countless players had already buckled under the pressure of facing him down the stretch. There was every reason to believe he'd be able to finish off the competition and add another green jacket to his wardrobe. However, prior success doesn't ensure future victory. Or, as Yogi Berra said, "It ain't over till it's over."

Samson is another strong man who took too much for granted.

Picture him in his little love nest with Delilah. He's all puffed up with the pride of a middle-aged man who's romancing a beautiful girl half his age. But she's no shrinking violet. Even for a girl so young, she's got all the moves. She's sophisticated beyond her years and knows how to get what she wants. Though the Bible says that Samson loved her, it's clear that she didn't reciprocate. To her, he was an amusing diversion, a fanciful lover, perhaps even a status symbol, but little more.

And then one day everything changed.

Samson became her winning lottery ticket.

The leaders of the Philistines approached her on the sly and asked her to find out how Samson could be subdued and captured. They each offered to pay her eleven hundred pieces of silver. It's difficult to say how much money this was because the value of a unit of silver fluctuated in biblical times. However, we do know that it was many times more than Abraham paid to buy a burial plot for his wife (Gen. 23:12–15), many times more than David paid Araunah for his threshing floor (2 Sam. 24:24), and many times more than Jeremiah paid to purchase a field (Jer. 32:9). It was also many times more than the amount the Old-Testament Law established as the price of a slave (Ex. 21:32). Clearly, Delilah was offered an enormous amount of money. So, like most people in her position would have done, she went right to work.

Her first three attempts to discover the secret of Samson's strength failed miserably. Each time she asked, he concocted a silly answer that she passed on to her Philistine handlers. They, in turn, rushed about, surreptitiously providing materials according to Samson's exact specifications—everything from bow strings to ropes to a loom—only to be foiled and fooled in the end. Every time he was bound, he broke free with a mere flex of his muscles.

Finally, Delilah decided to get serious and play the "You-don't-love-me" card. Judges 16:15–16 says she pouted and went on a relentless nagging campaign. At first Samson may have been amused, but her constant whining eventually began to wear him down. Finally, with his nerves completely shot, he gave in and told her his secret: "My hair has never been cut . . . for I was dedicated to God as a Nazirite from birth. If my head were shaved, my strength would leave me, and I would become as weak as anyone else" (Judg. 16:17).

Then the narrator makes an intriguing statement. He says, "Delilah realized he had finally told her the truth" (Judg. 16:18). Apparently, there was something in Samson's eyes or his demeanor that was different. Was it, perhaps, wistfulness? Was it a sense of sadness triggered by the mention of his long-forgotten vow? Is it possible that Samson, for a fleeting moment, felt the weight of his moral and spiritual failures pressing down on his soul? Might he have been, at that moment, as close to repentance as he had ever been in his adult life?

We'll never know. What we do know is that if such an emotion surfaced, it disappeared as quickly as it came, probably because Delilah's mood brightened instantly. Much to Samson's delight, the whining stopped, and she was suddenly back to her playful self. Perhaps she even rewarded Samson sexually for telling her the truth. It would have been a shrewd maneuver, setting him up perfectly for the final stage of her plan.

The scene that follows is one of the most famous in the Bible. Delilah, perhaps after an evening of heavy drinking and wild sex, managed to lull Samson to sleep with his head in her lap. I can see her stroking his magnificent hair and him luxuriating in the feel of her gentle touch. No doubt she waited for his muscles to relax and his breathing to settle into a gentle rhythm before signaling her co-conspirators. Quietly, they crept into the room and made their way to the bed. As she continued stroking his hair and massaging his scalp, they cut away strand after strand until, finally, both his hair and his strength were gone.

> THE LORD HAD LEFT HIM. . . . COULD THERE POSSIBLY BE A MORE CHILLING PHRASE?

To me, Judges 16:20 is the saddest of many sad verses in Samson's story:

> Then she cried out, "Samson! The Philistines have come to capture you!" When he woke up, he thought, "I will do as before and shake myself free." But he didn't realize the LORD had left him.

The Lord had left him. . . .

Could there possibly be a more chilling phrase?

But it isn't surprising. We could see it coming. Throughout his life, Samson took his greatest blessings for granted.

His parents.

His calling.

His vow.

His strength.

His security.

And his God.

Precious blessings one and all, yet they apparently never crossed Samson's mind. Things came so easy for him . . . he was so used to getting *what* he wanted, *when* he wanted it, that he rarely, if ever, gave a thought to the gifts that made it all possible. Or, more importantly, to the Giver of those gifts. He simply rode the wave, assuming it would never end. He assumed his reservoir of strength and ingenuity would never run dry. No doubt his plan was to live on the edge and then die of old age in the arms of a beautiful young woman.

But as Yogi says, "It ain't over till it's over."

In a matter of seconds . . .

Samson, who had cleverly tricked others, was completely bamboozled.

Samson, the ultimate free spirit, was taken prisoner.

Samson, who loved to ogle the ladies, had his eyes gouged out.

Samson, who had once terrified his enemies, was forced to entertain them.

Mark it down, my friend. Bad things happen to men who take too much for granted. Right now, you may be taking your wife for granted.

Or your kids.

Or your job.

Or your health.

Or your wealth.

Or your God.

Like Samson, you may have a track record of success that leads you to believe that these things will always be there for you when you need them. But believe me, if you don't cherish them, nurture them, monitor them, guard them, and demonstrate gratitude toward the one who gave them to you, you could easily lose them.

Many men already have.

That's why 1 Peter 5:8 says, "Be careful! Watch out for attacks from the Devil, your great enemy. He prowls around like a roaring lion, looking for some victim to devour." Obviously, Satan is looking for an unsuspecting victim. He's looking for someone who's cruising through life on autopilot, enjoying the ride, and taking his safety and his blessings for granted. He's looking for a victim of the Samson Syndrome.

> SATAN IS LOOKING FOR AN UNSUSPECTING VICTIM. HE'S LOOKING FOR SOMEONE WHO'S CRUISING THROUGH LIFE ON AUTOPILOT, ENJOYING THE RIDE, AND TAKING HIS SAFETY AND HIS BLESSINGS FOR GRANTED.

CHECK YOURSELF

It's imperative that you check yourself to see if you're guilty of taking too much for granted. The way you can do this is by honestly answering the following four questions. If you come to one you don't know how to answer, ask your spouse or a close, trusted friend. I suspect they'll be able to tell you the answer without any trouble at all.

Question #1: Are you given to periods of whining or complaining? A friend of mine used to complain about every aspect of his job. He hated driving so far to get to work. He didn't like his boss.

His coworkers got on his nerves. He said his office was too small and his computer needed to be upgraded. He even complained that they had a Pepsi machine in the break room when he preferred Coke!

And then one day he got laid off.

Suddenly, he was happy to drive even farther to get another job. And he started referring to his former coworkers as his friends. And *any* office—even a small office—sounded better than no office at all. It's amazing how a couple of missed paychecks completely changed his attitude! It made him appreciate the job he'd obviously started to take for granted.

What is it you're complaining about these days? Your job? Your wife? Your kids? How would you feel if one of those things was suddenly taken away from you?

Question #2: Is disobedience putting any of your blessings at risk? Recently, there was a story in the news about a preacher who was caught in a parked car with a prostitute. He insisted that he'd been trying to evangelize the woman and pleaded with her to corroborate his story. That's when he realized that she was, in fact, an undercover police officer. Rather than corroborating his story, the officer quipped, "If what the preacher was asking me to do had any connection with Christianity, I've got to believe there would be more people going to church."

> IS THERE SOMETHING ILLICIT GOING ON IN YOUR LIFE RIGHT NOW THAT WOULD DESTROY YOUR MOST PRECIOUS BLESSINGS IF IT WERE TO BECOME KNOWN?

Every day, countless strong men put their greatest blessings at risk by indulging in sin. They risk their marriages, their jobs, their reputations, their health, and even their hopes and dreams, all for a few moments of pleasure. And when they do, they're leaving no doubt that they've begun to take those blessings for granted.

What about you? Is there something illicit going on in your life right now that would destroy your most precious blessings if it were to become known?

Question #3: Does the grass always look greener on the other side of the fence?

I read a letter to an advice columnist a while back from a lady whose husband was about to drive her crazy. She said they had moved fourteen times during the twelve years of their marriage. They had lived in fourteen different communities and seven different states, all because her husband was never satisfied. He always believed there was another job out there that would be just a little bit better than the one he had. The kicker was that, after fourteen moves, he was back to making the same salary he'd made on his very first job!

It's so sad that some people live their entire lives for what's on the other side of the fence and never appreciate the green, green grass of home. Where have your eyes been focused recently?

Question #4: Do you practice good health habits? I read recently that there are two million people in America who have glaucoma, but only half of them are aware of it because so few people get their eyes checked on a regular basis. We take our eyesight and lots of other health-related issues for granted. Have you had your cholesterol checked lately? Or your blood pressure? And strong man, how long has it been since you had a colonoscopy? Did you know that colon cancer is one of the most common and deadly forms of cancer in men? After you turn forty, you should start having your colon checked on a regular basis, especially if you have a family history of colon cancer.

Amazingly, there are countless men who never go to the doctor. One guy even told me, "The only way I'm going to the doctor is if they haul me in on a stretcher." I responded, "If you wait that long, they may just bypass the doctor's office and head straight for the morgue."

If any of these questions produced a little twinge of guilt, then you may indeed be taking too much for granted. And if that's the case, then you need to take the next step.

CHANGE YOURSELF

There are essentially two ways you can be transformed into a person who takes note of God's blessings and appreciates them. One is the *hard* way and the other is the *easy* way. The hard way has to do with crashing and burning and is illustrated by the prodigal son (Luke 15:11–32). He gave little thought to his blessings and wound up squandering his inheritance. Only after he hit rock bottom did he realize how foolish he'd been.

> STRONG MEN ARE, BY NATURE, CLIMBERS. THEY TEND TO LIVE WITH AN UPWARD TILT TO THEIR CHINS, AND FOR THAT REASON, SOMETIMES FAIL TO TAKE NOTE OF THE PEOPLE AROUND THEM.

Thankfully, there's a much easier way to make this transformation. Let me suggest three things you can do that will help you avoid this aspect of the Samson Syndrome and start appreciating the good things God has given you.

First, take a closer look at the people around you. Strong men are, by nature, climbers. They tend to live with an upward tilt to their chins, and for that reason, sometimes fail to take note of the people around them.

A number of years ago I was driving through southern Indiana in the fall and happened to see something that almost made me run off the road. I blinked hard a couple of times and actually doubled back to see if I really saw what I thought I saw. A man was in his front yard raking leaves. It was a huge yard, and he had obviously been at it for hours. He had raked up a half dozen large piles and appeared to be ready to start bagging or burning them. The thing that made the scene surreal was the fact that the man was in a wheelchair and had no legs.

I remember being in awe of that man.

And I remember being ashamed of myself.

You see, I had recently had knee surgery. I tore my anterior cruciate ligament in a church-league basketball game and was forced to hobble around on crutches for a few weeks. I had complained about the inconvenience and whined about being knocked out of action for the entire basketball season. I have often wondered if God set it up for me to drive by and see that guy raking leaves just to wake me up and snap me to my senses. If He did, it worked.

Strong man, pull your head down out of the clouds and look around. You'll see people everywhere who are battling hardships that you have probably never had to face. Visit a nursing home or a hospital. Better yet, go to a children's hospital. Take a look at the youngsters whose dreams are never going to come true. While you're fighting for your next raise or promotion, they're fighting for another day of life. While you're complaining about some minor inconvenience, they're just happy to see another sunrise. Take a closer look at the people around you.

Second, take life a little slower. I'm convinced that much of the ingratitude demonstrated by Christians could be more accurately labeled "forgetfulness." It's not that we aren't grateful for our blessings. It's more that our lives are so busy and fast-paced that we forget to think about our blessings and thank God for them. Might this have been the problem of the nine lepers Jesus healed who never returned to thank Him (Luke 17:11–19)? As former outcasts, were they suddenly so anxious to see their families and friends that they took off at a dead run and simply forgot to return and thank the Lord?

Recently, Marilyn and I returned from a trip to Gatlinburg, Tennessee. We rented a beautiful chalet that was perched on the side of a small mountain. All we could see as we looked out over the balcony was a little one-lane road disappearing into a dense forest. It was dead quiet except for the chirping of birds and the rustling of leaves. It seemed as if we were cut off from the outside world.

Every time I find myself in such a place, I sense a kind of reawakening of my spiritual senses. I am less stressed. I am more observant and appreciative of God's magnificent creation. I have more time to read and pray and reflect on my life and my blessings without constantly being interrupted. I can certainly understand why we often read about Jesus seeking out a secluded place to pray and spend time alone with his disciples.

> YOU NEED TO FIND A PLACE WHERE GOD'S "STILL SMALL VOICE" IS NOT DROWNED OUT BY CHIRPING CELL PHONES, HONKING HORNS, AND BLARING MUSIC.

Now, I am not suggesting that you check out of the human race and go live in a cave. However, as a strong man, you probably do need to slow down a bit. You probably need to create some opportunities, not just for rest and relaxation, but for quiet reflection. You need to find a place where God's "still small voice" is not drowned out by chirping cell phones, honking horns, and blaring music. And when you find such a place, you need to visit it often. It may be on a mountain in Gatlinburg, or in a rocking chair in your guest bedroom. The location isn't important, as long as the place and the time you spend there help you reconnect with what's important in life.

Third, dare to associate with people whose lives are different from yours. A few years ago I went to Haiti on a short-term mission trip. Simply put, that trip changed my life. When I got home, I couldn't sit down to a steak or a plate of spaghetti without thinking of the people I met in Haiti who lived every day on a slim helping of beans and rice and whatever fruit they could pull off a tree limb. When I went shopping, I couldn't buy a shirt without thinking of the children who ran naked through the streets of the tiny village where we were working. When I took a hot shower, I couldn't stop thinking about the Haitian women who washed themselves, their dishes, and their clothes in the same babbling brook that was used as a latrine. When I flipped on a light or clicked on the television, I remembered how my new Haitian friends were given only about thirty minutes of electricity a day. And when I cashed my paycheck, I thought about the 90-percent unemployment rate in Haiti and how the vast majority of Haitian citizens will never see as much money as I make in a single week.

I know that not everyone will have the means or the opportunity to go on a mission trip to a Third-World country. But there are other ways you can connect with those whose lives are very different from yours. My brother, Phil, for example, who is a highly respected college professor, decided to become a Big Brother several years ago. He "adopted" a troubled teenage boy who came from a broken home. The boy's mother was often drunk and welcomed a parade of strange men into her home and her bed. Phil stuck with the boy through some very hard times and even fixed up a spare bedroom so the boy would have a place to stay when things became unbearable at home. The one thing Phil said to me that I'll always remember is that Big Brothering gave him a greater appreciation for his own family and home life.

How could you connect with people whose lives are different from yours? Maybe you could become a Big Brother or Sister. Maybe you could do volunteer work with the Boy Scouts or the Little League. Maybe there's a benevolence ministry at your church that reaches out to people in need. I'm guessing that if you got involved in any such program or ministry, you'd soon be thanking God for some blessings long overlooked.

As I close this chapter, I can't help but think of one of the strongest men of all time, baseball's Lou Gehrig. You don't play 2,130 consecutive games in the big leagues and get the nickname "Iron Horse" if you aren't strong. Yet Lou Gehrig never took the good things of life for granted. Even after he was diagnosed with Amyotrophic Lateral Sclerosis (ALS), a rare and deadly disease that would eventually bear his name, he never lost sight of the wonderful blessings that were his to enjoy. Read again the words he spoke at Yankee Stadium on July 4, 1939, as he stood before sixty-thousand fans.

> Fans, for the past two weeks you have been reading about
> a bad break I got. Yet, today I consider myself the lucki-

est man on the face of the earth. I have been in ballparks for seventeen years and have never received anything but kindness and encouragement from you fans. Look at these grand men. Which of you wouldn't consider it the highlight of his career to associate with them for even one day? Sure, I'm lucky. Who wouldn't consider it an honor to have known Jacob Ruppert? Also, the builder of baseball's greatest empire, Ed Barrow? Or to have spent the next nine years with that wonderful little fellow, Miller Huggins? Then to have spent the next nine years with that outstanding leader, that smart student of psychology, the best manager in baseball today, Joe McCarthy?

Sure, I'm lucky. When the New York Giants, a team you would give your right arm to beat, and vice versa, sends you a gift, that's something! When everybody down to the groundskeepers and those boys in the white coats remember you with trophies, that's something! When you have a wonderful mother-in-law who takes sides with you in squabbles against her own daughter, that's something! When you have a father and mother who work all their lives so that you can have an education and build your body, it's a blessing! When you have a wife who has been a tower of strength and shown more courage than you dreamed existed, that's the finest I know.

So I close in saying that I might have had a tough break, but I have an awful lot to live for!

On June 2, 1941, less than two years after his unforgettable speech at Yankee Stadium, the Iron Horse died. He left behind a .340 lifetime batting average, 493 home runs, and 1,990 runs batted in. But his most worthy contribution to the human race has nothing to do with baseball. In a world full of Samsons, Lou Gehrig reminds us that strong men can indeed be humble and grateful.

TWELVE

STRONG MEN TEND TO LOSE SIGHT OF THE BIG PICTURE

All men should try to learn
before they die
what they are running from,
and to, and why.

—JAMES THURBER

But I have this complaint against you. You don't love me or
each other as you did at first.

—JESUS CHRIST (REVELATION 2:4)

THE BIBLICAL ACCOUNT OF SAMSON'S LIFE PILES ONE spectacular scene on top of another. In fact, there is a sort of crescendo to his story. You can feel it building as you read. You just know that a man who has been involved in so many hair-raising escapades is going to go out in a blaze of glory.

And does he ever.

After capturing and blinding him, the Philistines took Samson to Gaza, stuck him in a prison, and put him to work grinding flour. You have to give them credit. With a little ingenuity and a generous helping of female charm, they did what many would have said was impossible: They captured the ultimate free spirit. They eliminated their public enemy number one. Unfortunately for them, they then turned around and made one of the biggest blunders in the history of mankind: They forgot to keep cutting Samson's hair. This would be like the U.S. capturing Osama bin Laden and then forgetting to lock the door of his prison cell!

As a result, Judges 16:22 is one of the few optimistic verses in the entire account of Samson's life. It's like finding a pool of fresh water in the desert. After filling us in on the sickening details of Samson's arrest and torture, the narrator says, "But before long his hair began to grow back." And with that statement, we know it's time to fasten our seatbelts. The ride has been wild for sure, but somehow we sense that we haven't seen anything yet. The final loop on this roller coaster is going to be a doozy.

Ironically, it all came to a head at a party. Samson, whose whole life had been one big party, suddenly found himself being dragged in front of his captors. They guzzled their booze and howled with laughter as he staggered and flopped about like a bad slapstick comedian. Finally, with the help of a compassionate servant, he found his bearings between two pillars. He knew he was in the center of the temple and that pillars in such a location would provide support for the entire roof.

Suddenly, there seemed only one thing to do.

Samson turned his blind eyes toward heaven and spoke to the same God he had pretty much ignored throughout his life:

> "Sovereign LORD, remember me again. O God, please strengthen me one more time so that I may pay back the Philistines for the loss of my eyes." Then Samson put his hands on the center pillars of the temple and pushed

against them with all his might. "Let me die with the Philistines," he prayed. And the temple crashed down on the Philistine leaders and all the people. So he killed more people when he died than he had during his entire lifetime. (Judg. 16:28–30)

Throughout the writing of this book I asked quite a few lay people to give me their off-the-cuff impressions of Samson. By far, the most common response was, "He made a lot of mistakes, but at least he finished well." I also found that to be a common sentiment among a number of writers and preachers. The feeling apparently is that since Samson sacrificed his life to wipe out a multitude of Philistines and died with a prayer on his lips, he must have gotten his act together at the very end.

I disagree.

It's my conviction that Samson had few, if any, other options as he stood before the Philistine leaders. Even with his strength returning, he was still blind, which made it impossible for him to plan an escape, let alone attempt one. He also knew that his heartless captors would never grow tired of mistreating and humiliating him. Their cruelty had never known any limits, and it would surely be spurred to new heights of creativity as the months and years passed. Simply put, Samson knew he was doomed to a life of misery. It's only natural that he would consider suicide.

But there's an even more compelling argument for my position.

Look closely at Samson's prayer.

Do you see any words of repentance?

Do you see any evidence that Samson regretted his many mistakes?

Do you see any indication that Samson even *understood* his mistakes?

No, you don't. Instead, you see a man who hadn't changed a bit. After a lifetime of "me-first" living, Samson was still preoccupied with himself. Notice all the personal pronouns in his prayer:

> . . . remember *me* again . . .
> . . . please strengthen *me* . . .
> . . . so that *I* may pay back the Philistines . . .
> . . . for the loss of *my* eyes . . .
> . . . let *me* die with the Philistines . . .

Sadly, Samson ended his life the way he had lived it: selfishly. His actions were not born out of a heroic desire to fulfill his life's calling. They were simply an attempt to get revenge. He wasn't pushing against those pillars because he loved God. He was pushing against them because he hated his Philistine captors and wanted to pay them back for gouging out his eyes. After a lifetime of matching wits, they had pulled a fast one on him and he was bound and determined to have the last laugh. Even if it meant taking his own life.

And here we come face-to-face with what may well have been Samson's biggest problem of all: He completely lost sight of the big picture.

Think about it.

From day one, Samson's mission was clearly stated. He was to "rescue Israel from the Philistines" (Judg. 13:5). He was to get them fired up and organized and to lead a crushing revolt that would set them free and eliminate the Philistine threat against God's people forever. But he didn't do it. As far as we know, he didn't even try. The best we can say for Samson is that he carried on a lifelong feud with the Philistines. He aggravated and frustrated them. He killed a few of them here and there. He made them look foolish at times. But he never did the one big thing he was supposed to do. He never pulled the Israelites together and wiped them out.

To be honest, I've been dreading the writing of this chapter because I knew it was going to sting. While I struggle with a few of the tendencies that make up the Samson Syndrome, none of them hit me harder than this one. On many occasions I, too, have lost sight of the big picture. I have found myself veering off on tangents and obsessing over side issues that had nothing to do with God's ultimate will for my life. I have allowed my time and attention to be eaten up by tasks that seemed important at the moment, but carried no real or lasting significance. I have stressed out over problems that were completely beyond my ability to solve. I have been guilty of ignoring the people who love me most and allowing the people who don't love me at all to monopolize my time and drain my energy. And I hate to admit it, but like Samson, I have even allowed myself to get sucked into foolish competitions with my peers.

Writing this book has helped me understand how important the big picture is, how hard Satan tries to draw a strong man's attention away from it, and how good he is at getting the job done. Think of it: He managed to distract Samson for his entire life! *Never* did Samson tune in to the big picture and set about the business of fulfilling his calling.

If you're a strong man, you need to understand that Satan will try to do to you just what he did to Samson. In a variety of ways, he'll try to keep you from focusing on the big picture.

THE TIES THAT BLIND

I once heard an old preacher say, "Life is hard, but at least it's not complicated." That's what Solomon was driving at in Ecclesiastes 1:9 where he said "History merely repeats itself. It has all been done before. Nothing under the sun is truly new." How true. After all these centuries, Satan is still using the same four blinders in his attempt to keep strong men from focusing on the big picture.

Blinder #1: PLEASURE. Many years ago the small church I was serving was preparing to hire its first secretary. I called a few preachers and asked for their input regarding the job description and the type of person we should look for. I'll never forget what one fellow said: "Mark, do yourself a favor and hire someone real homely. You'll get a lot more work done if you do."

Let me be quick to say (in case any of my former secretaries read this) that I have *never* made homeliness a requirement for employment. Obviously, my friend was speaking tongue in cheek to make a point. Few things are more distracting to a man than an attractive member of the opposite sex.

There's an old joke about two preachers who took a day off and went to the beach to relax. All day long they watched as one gorgeous, bikini-clad female after another went sauntering by. Finally, one of the preachers said, "That's it, I give up. I just can't do it anymore. I've got to quit."

The second preacher said, "You mean quit coming to the beach?"

"No, I mean quit the ministry."

A story like that is intended to produce a chuckle, but it's hard to laugh when you have friends who've actually quit the ministry (or their marriages) because of a longing for worldly pleasure.

But of course, it's not just preachers and it's not just sexual temptation. Every man finds pleasure in something. It could be something good like golf, or bad like alcohol. Rest assured that Satan will identify your greatest source of pleasure—good or bad—and try his best to get you too wrapped up in it.

Blinder #2: PAIN. While Satan kept sending a steady stream of beautiful women into Samson's line of sight, he took a completely different approach with Job: He pummeled him with one painful blow after another. Joseph also got kicked in the teeth. So did David and the Old-Testament

> REST ASSURED THAT SATAN WILL IDENTIFY YOUR GREATEST SOURCE OF PLEASURE—GOOD OR BAD—AND TRY HIS BEST TO GET YOU TOO WRAPPED UP IN IT.

prophets and Paul. In fact, listen to the *crack* of whips and the *thud* of stones bouncing off of Paul's body as you read these words:

> I have . . . been whipped times without number, and faced death again and again. Five different times the Jews gave me thirty-nine lashes. Three times I was beaten with rods. Once I was stoned. Three times I was shipwrecked. Once I spent a whole night and a day adrift at sea. I have traveled many weary miles. I have faced danger from flooded rivers and from robbers. I have faced danger from my own people, the Jews, as well as from the Gentiles. I have faced danger in the cities, in the deserts, and on the stormy seas. And I have faced danger from men who claim to be Christians but are not. I have lived with weariness and pain and sleepless nights. Often I have been hungry and thirsty and have gone without food. Often I have shivered with

cold, without enough clothing to keep me warm. (2 Cor.
11:23–27)

You have to give Satan credit for being persistent. He obviously believed his best chance to distract Paul was through pain and discomfort, so he really poured it on. Thankfully, Paul didn't get off track, but many men do.

Recently, a friend came to my office for a chat. I knew that he'd been going through some struggles, including the loss of a job, financial stress, and even some health issues. To his credit, he didn't try to blame God for his problems. But he did ask an interesting question: "Why do you think Satan spends so much time hammering me?"

I hate loaded questions like that, but in this case, I found some ready words on my lips. I said, "I don't know, but have you considered that maybe he's found a chink in your spiritual armor? You're a nice, hard-working guy, a devoted husband and father, and I know you love the Lord. But in all honesty, I notice that when something bad happens, you start veering off track, spiritually. You miss church for two or three weeks, you don't show up for meetings, and you get irritable. Then when things improve, you get back on track. I hate to say this, but if I were Satan, I'd hammer you too. It works."

I could tell my words stung him a little, but he didn't deny them. Since then, I've noticed that he's trying a lot harder to stay spiritually focused when things get hard. And maybe it's just my imagination, but it sure seems as if the hammering has let up.

Blinder #3: PROSPERITY. If you're a baseball fan, you probably remember a very strange incident that happened during spring training in 2002. Ruben Rivera, an outfielder for the New

York Yankees, was caught stealing a bat and glove from team-mate Derek Jeter's locker. He'd struck a deal with a memorabilia dealer to provide the items for twenty-five hundred dollars. What boggles the mind is the fact that Rivera, a journeyman outfielder, had signed a million-dollar contract with the Yankees and was having a fabulous spring. A career .218 hitter, he was hitting .350 at the time of the incident and had a great chance of mak-ing the Yankees' opening day roster. Instead, when the theft was discovered, he was given his outright release.

Talk about losing sight of the big picture!

When I heard that incident reported on the news, I immedi-ately thought of Paul's words in 1 Timothy 6:10: "For the love of money is at the root of all kinds of evil. And some people, craving money, have wandered from the faith and pierced themselves with many sorrows." The world is full of people who have been blinded by the lure of prosperity.

Blinder #4: POWER. It was Lord Acton who said, "Power cor-rupts, and absolute power corrupts absolutely." In Scripture, no one illustrates this better than King Saul.

The first thing we learn about Saul is that he was the tallest and most handsome young man in Israel (1 Sam. 9:2). That alone would be a prescription for arrogance in most people, but Saul was surprisingly humble and steered clear of the limelight. In fact, on the day that he was to be anointed king by Samuel, he was nowhere to be found. A thorough search of the area finally turned him up hiding behind some baggage (1 Sam. 10:20–23). Even at the age of thirty, he was apparently so self-conscious that he just didn't feel comfortable parading in front of all the people.

But a taste of power changed everything. With every passing year, Saul became more arrogant and more hateful toward anyone he thought might be stealing his glory. The ultimate example of his blindness to the big picture is seen in his jealous obsession with David. You'll remember that David had killed Goliath and won immediate fame. People were so impressed with David's courage and skill that they even began singing folk songs about him, which was more than Saul could stand. He was so infuriated by David's popularity that he spent years chasing him all over the countryside and paid no attention to his real enemies, the Philistines. Not surprisingly, the Philistines eventually attacked and caught the Israelite army in a state of disarray. Saul and his sons, along with many Israelite soldiers, were killed (1 Sam. 31).

A few years ago I was part of a group of preachers that met with a Florida politician who was just concluding his first term in office and seeking reelection. During that meeting, someone asked him what surprised him most about living and working in Washington, D.C. He said, "I didn't realize how seductive it would be. When you live among those great monuments and rub shoulders every day with the world's most powerful people, it can really go to your head."

Pleasure.

Pain.

Prosperity.

And power.

Have any of these things caused you to veer off track? Think back to the days when you were just starting your family or your career. Were there goals you were determined to reach? Were there priorities you were determined to maintain throughout your life? Was there a calling on your life that you felt would guide you forever? If so, how are you doing now in relation to those things? Are you still on track? Can you honestly say that you've made progress? Or did you make a wrong turn somewhere?

GETTING BACK ON TRACK

At the Disney World Resort, there is a miniature-golf complex called Winter-Summerland, which has two courses side by side. One is designed to make you feel as though you're playing in the tropics and the other has the look of the North Pole. The first time I played there, I had my game face on. Most of the miniature-golf courses in this area are very difficult, and I assumed Disney's would be no different. I was prepared to do battle with tunnels and windmills and waterfalls and crazy bank shots. As it turned out, I played the best game of my life. Believe it or not, I made ten holes-in-one! As the saying goes, I must have been butter because I was on a roll! After aces on the first three holes, I was strutting like a peacock, doing my end-zone dance and humming the theme from *Rocky*. However, it was hard for me to enjoy my success, because everyone else was doing just as well. Even a little kid we were playing with was whacking the ball blindly in the general direction of the hole and making ace after ace.

On about the fourth hole I knelt down and took a knee-high look at the "fairway." As I suspected, it had been molded and shaped to funnel the ball toward and into the hole. It wasn't noticeable if you were standing up, but from the proper angle you could see that there was a "flow" to every hole that carried your ball in the right direction. I discovered later that the course had been designed to be child friendly. While most miniature-golf courses are confounding to adults and impossible for children, this was intended to be one where the kids could play and enjoy the thrill of seeing the ball drop into the cup.

I believe it's possible to design your life in a similar fashion. I believe it's possible to create a lifestyle that flows in the right direction and keeps you from getting off track or losing sight of the big picture. Let me offer some ideas that will help you do this.

First, write a personal mission statement. Most successful businesses and churches have crafted mission statements that are designed to keep the organization on target. At PCC, our mission statement reads as follows:

> Poinciana Christian Church exists to advance the cause of Christ through worship, ministry, education, and fellowship.

It's simple, but effective. In our leadership meetings, all new ideas and proposals are evaluated in the light of that statement. If it doesn't advance the cause of Christ, and if it doesn't fit under the heading of worship, ministry, education, or fellowship, we don't do it. That doesn't mean the idea or proposal is necessarily bad. It may be quite worthwhile, in fact. But we can't do everything, so we have chosen to concentrate on those things that squarely fit our mission.

Have you ever thought about writing a *personal* mission statement? A while back I decided that it would be good for me to do just that, so I gave it some thought, and this is what I came up with:

> Each day I will give my Creator the very best that I have to offer.

I will keep my feet on the path of righteousness,
My hands busy with good works,
My heart soft toward those in need,
And my eyes on eternity.

Obviously, some days I'm more successful than others at fulfilling my personal mission statement. But that's not the point. The point is that my mission statement keeps me on course.

If you've been known to veer off and get sidetracked in life, why not take some time and think about what your ultimate purpose is? Pray about it. Consider your passions, your talents, and God's will for your life. Then, as it begins to take shape in your mind, define it in very specific terms and write it down. You might have to tinker with it for a while until you get it just right. When you finally have it the way you want it, memorize it and stick it in places where you'll see it, such as your bathroom mirror, the dash of your car, or your computer monitor. It's uncanny how a single statement can snap you back to reality when you feel yourself starting to drift off course.

Second, choose friends that understand and support your life goals. As I've already pointed out, this is one of the most troubling aspects of Samson's life. As far as we know, he had no close friends among his own people. He didn't leave room in his life for anyone who could have acted as a mentor or spiritual advisor. Instead, he was almost constantly in the company of the enemy, the very people who stood to benefit if he got off track and lost sight of his purpose in life.

Marilyn and I are fans of the Biography Channel. We love to watch the documentaries and learn little-known facts about famous and successful people. One thing I've noticed as I've watched these programs is that people who achieve true greatness in this world almost always have a strong supporting cast. They may come out of poverty. They may start life with all kinds of disadvantages. But at some point, usually at an early age, they get connected with supportive people who believe in them and are willing to help them in the pursuit of their goals. It is true that "as iron sharpens iron, a friend sharpens a friend" (Prov. 27:17).

Let me encourage you to take a careful inventory of your friends and associates. Go through the names one at a time and honestly evaluate the impact they're having on your life. Ask yourself who's helping to channel you in the direction of your true purpose, and who isn't. And when you see the truth, don't be afraid of it. Have the courage to exercise discretion in those relationships. Draw closer to the people who are helping you stay on the right road and keep your distance from those who tend to lead you astray.

Third, learn to tell the difference between the urgent and the important. Every day a hefty stack of mail arrives at our offices. Many of those envelopes are addressed to me and stamped with the words *Important!, Urgent!,* or *Dated Material!* A recent one even said across the bottom of the envelope: "You'll be sorry if you don't read this!"

> DRAW CLOSER TO THE PEOPLE WHO ARE HELPING YOU STAY ON THE RIGHT ROAD AND KEEP YOUR DISTANCE FROM THOSE WHO TEND TO LEAD YOU ASTRAY.

That's odd because I didn't read it, and I've yet to feel sorry.

The point is that in our hectic, fast-paced world, everything screams to be done right this instant. But the truth is that some of those things don't need to be done at all! Just as the vast majority of envelopes I receive contain nothing pertinent to my life and work, so many of the demands that people try to place on me offer nothing beneficial to my ministry. They may be important to *someone*, but they aren't necessarily relevant to what *I'm* trying to accomplish. All they would do for me is drain my energy and eat up my valuable time.

And take me away from my true purpose.

Fourth, work hard to develop and maintain an eternal perspective. I'm sure you've seen the GodSpeaks billboards as you've traveled around the country.

IN OUR HECTIC, FAST-PACED WORLD, EVERYTHING SCREAMS TO BE DONE RIGHT THIS INSTANT. BUT THE TRUTH IS THAT SOME OF THOSE THINGS DON'T NEED TO BE DONE AT ALL!

They're big black signs with plain white letters containing messages from God. Well, maybe not exactly from God, but from some clever people who want you and me to think more about him. Here are a few of the sayings:

- We need to talk.
- Big Bang Theory? You've got to be kidding.
- What part of "you shall not" don't you understand?
- Loved the wedding! Now invite me to the marriage.
- Let's meet at my house Sunday before the game.
- You think it's hot here.
- That "love thy neighbor" thing? I meant it.
- Have you read my #1 bestseller? (There will be a test.)
- Don't make me come down there.

As of this writing, the GodSpeaks campaign has put up ten thousand billboards in two hundred cities across America and has plans to expand into several foreign countries. It's been featured in countless newspaper articles and special news reports on NBC, CBS, ABC, CNN, and MSNBC. The campaign has also printed the sayings on T-shirts, coffee mugs, license plates, key chains, bumper stickers, magnets, ball caps, and wall plaques.

Some people—even a lot of Christians—are very critical of this campaign. They say that no one should put words in God's mouth, and they object to the commercialization of God's name. I appreciate those concerns, but at the same time, I can't help feeling that anything that makes us cast an eye toward God and eternity can't be all bad. Paul said, "Let heaven fill your thoughts. Do not think only about things down here on earth" (Col. 3:2).

That, in a nutshell, may have been Samson's biggest mistake. He simply never looked up. He allowed himself to become completely wrapped up in the people and pleasures of this world.

Strong man, be careful.

You live and work in this world.

You're seeking to make your mark on this world.

You're stretching yourself to meet and exceed the world's expectations.

You're finding satisfaction in the worldly success you're able to achieve.

Fine.

Just don't lose sight of the big picture.

Don't forget to look up.

Don't forget that this world isn't all there is.

Don't forget to plan for eternity.

I can think of no greater tragedy than for a man to gain the whole world and lose his soul.

EPILOGUE

SURPRISINGLY, SAMSON'S STORY DOESN'T END IN THE rubble of a Philistine temple, but all the way over in the book of Hebrews. We find his name tucked into a long list of great Bible heroes. People who, by faith, "overthrew kingdoms, ruled with justice, and received what God had promised them" (Heb. 11:33). You might think that Samson's appearance in such a list indicates a greater degree of faith and obedience than I've given him credit for in this book.

Maybe he wasn't such a bad guy after all.

Maybe he was just misunderstood.

Maybe the writer of Judges didn't give him a fair shake.

I happen to think Samson was every bit as incorrigible as the text would lead us to believe. The fact that he shows up in Hebrews 11 is in no way a tribute to him. Rather, it's a tribute to God's grace. Having spent the last year of my life in a detailed study of Samson's story, I can honestly say that I stand in awe of a God who is gracious enough to tolerate a guy like Samson, let alone use him. If I had been calling the shots, I probably would have blown Samson off somewhere around his twenty-fifth birthday. I would have grown completely frustrated and found another person to work through. Someone who would take the Nazirite vow seriously. Someone who would follow orders.

But God stuck with Samson, and in doing so, confirmed what Daniel said: "The Lord our God is merciful and forgiving, even though we have rebelled against him" (Dan. 9:9). Of course, there's always the chance that someone might read Samson's story and feel emboldened to disobey God. A man might say, "If Samson can fool around and still be saved, why can't I?" But anyone who would adopt such an attitude is probably going to sin anyway and is only looking for a rationalization.

> EVEN IF HE DOES SHOW UP IN HEBREWS 11, SAMSON'S LIFE IS STILL A STUDY IN MISSED OPPORTUNITIES. PERHAPS NO ONE IN THE ENTIRE BIBLE DID SO LITTLE WITH SO MUCH.

As you lay this book down for what may be the final time, I'd like for you to think, not so much about what Samson did, but about what he *could* have done. Even if he does show up in Hebrews 11, Samson's life is still a study in missed opportunities. Perhaps no one in the entire Bible did so little with so much.

In the end, I wrote this book because I believe there's a little Samson in all of us. Face it, guys. With God's help, we're capable of such great things. But we're never more than one bad choice away from humiliation. That's a scary thought, isn't it? By this time tomorrow any one of us could be broken and devastated by sin. But it doesn't have to happen. By understanding who we are and the subtle tendencies we face . . . and by committing ourselves wholly to the God who called us to serve Him, we can fulfill our calling and be faithful unto death.

STUDY QUESTIONS
FOR PERSONAL REFLECTION OR GROUP DISCUSSION

I HAVE PREPARED THIS SECTION FOR THOSE WHO LIKE TO go a little beyond the printed text of a book. If you enjoy exploring the nooks and crannies of your heart, these questions are designed to assist you. You will notice that some of the questions will require you to delve into some very personal areas. If you're using this study guide with a group, I would suggest that you be judicious in what you share. While it is very helpful to participate in a candid discussion with other Christians, it is also unwise and unnecessary to reveal extremely personal information that would prove embarrassing to yourself or others.

CHAPTER ONE: STRONG MEN TEND TO DISREGARD BOUNDARIES

1. Name some boundaries that society imposes on the average adult. Which of these do you find to be the most frustrating? Why?

2. Are there any boundaries in your life that are self-imposed? What are they? Why did you set them up? Have they accomplished what you hoped they would?

3. The Nazirite Vow was commonly taken for a period of thirty or sixty days by people who had a desire for a deeper, more intimate connection with God. How would you feel about undertaking an intensive program of self-discipline and personal sacrifice for two months? Would you be willing to give up television? Movies? Secular music? Red meat? Junk food? Secular literature?

4. Are there any "fences" in your life that you have allowed to fall into disrepair? What immediate steps can you take to start getting them back in shape?

5. It's often said that the grass always looks greener on the other side of the fence. Can you think of a time when you climbed over a fence in search of greener grass, only to realize later that you made a mistake?

CHAPTER TWO: STRONG MEN TEND TO STRUGGLE WITH LUST

1. Webster defines lust as "excessive" sexual desire. In your opinion, at what point does sexual desire cross the line and become excessive? Specifically, what behaviors do you consider to be out of bounds for the Christian? What Scriptures can you point to that support your ideas?

2. Samson's parents tried to convince him not to marry the girl from Timnah, but the intensity of his desire caused him to turn a deaf ear. What are some things parents can do while their children are still young and impressionable to make sure they are well equipped to honor God with their sexuality?

3. Samson's parents eventually gave in and supported his desire to marry the girl from Timnah. Should they have done this? Is there ever a time when parents should disassociate themselves from the actions of their children? If so, give some examples.

4. Humans are the only creatures on earth that are capable of understanding and enjoying romance. What does this imply? When was the last time you did something thoughtful and romantic for your wife that had nothing to do with sex? What could you do to fan the flames of romance that you have never done before?

5. Paul told Timothy to "run from anything that stimulates youthful lust" (2 Tim. 2:22). What stimulates youthful lust in one person may not affect someone else. What stimulates youthful lust in you? What can you do to separate yourself from those things?

CHAPTER THREE: STRONG MEN TEND TO IGNORE GOOD ADVICE

1. What's the best piece of advice you ever received? Who gave it to you? How do you feel it has impacted your life?

2. Can you think of some good advice you rejected? Who gave it to you? How have you suffered as a result?

3. Strong men like Samson are notoriously stubborn. The old joke is that a man can be lost for hours but will refuse to stop and ask for directions. In your opinion, what is it about strong men that makes them so stubborn?

4. Moses had Jethro. Tiger Woods has Butch Harmon. Even someone as smart as the President of the United States has a team of advisors. Is there anyone in your life that you depend

on to give you counsel? If not, can you think of someone who might be able and willing to fulfill that role?

5. Is there a person in your life that you have trouble taking advice from, even though you know he/she is very wise? If so, why do you resist that person's counsel?

6. Is there someone who has trouble taking advice from you, even though you have valuable insights to offer? If so, what can you do to make yourself and your advice more acceptable?

CHAPTER FOUR: STRONG MEN TEND TO BREAK RULES

1. When Samson dipped his hand into the carcass of the lion and scooped up some honey, he broke the rules of his Nazirite vow. Does the fact that no one was there to see him do it mitigate the circumstances at all? Are all sins created equal?

2. Most people consider Samson's sexual sins to be his most grievous. What made the scooping of the honey particularly insidious? Can you name some harmless-looking sins that are destroying men's lives today?

3. While you were growing up, who imposed the most rules on you? A parent? Teacher? Guardian? Coach? How did you feel about that person while you were under his/her authority? How do you feel about that person today? In what ways have you benefited from his/her influence?

4. Have you ever knowingly broken a rule because you felt it was in conflict with God's will? Did you suffer for that decision? In what way? Would you do it again?

5. Is there a rule you're being forced to follow (perhaps at work) that you find oppressive? What is it? Can you see any purpose

STUDY QUESTIONS

for the rule? If you were going to try to get the rule changed, how could you do it without compromising your faith?

CHAPTER FIVE: STRONG MEN TEND TO OVERESTIMATE THEIR OWN CLEVERNESS

1. Have you ever done something that seemed like a good idea at the time, but turned out to be incredibly foolish? What was it? How did you suffer as a result?

2. The seven enemies of discernment are pride, liquor, anger, lust, greed, hatred, and impatience. Which of these were involved in Samson's foolish bet with his Philistine groomsmen? Which of these have tripped you up in the past? What steps have you taken to make sure they don't trip you up again?

3. Samson repeatedly made poor choices in two areas: He chose to hang out with the wrong people and he didn't control his sexual desire. Is there an area (or maybe more than one) where you have made repeated mistakes? Why do you think that is? What can you do to change that pattern?

4. Have you ever lost something precious because of a foolish choice? What was it? How has that loss impacted your life? Is there any way you can reclaim that blessing? If so, what would it take?

CHAPTER SIX: STRONG MEN TEND TO USE ANGER AS A TOOL

1. Think about some times when you have been extremely angry. What did you do? When your anger subsided, did you feel guilty? Did you find yourself having to make apologies?

197

2. Samson was angry because he was embarrassed by his Philistine groomsmen. What makes you angrier, being embarrassed or seeing injustice being done to someone else? In what way and to what extent does the object of your anger shed light on your character?

3. Have you ever used anger as a tool? Perhaps to control and intimidate your employees or your family members? If so, think about those people right now. How would you describe their feelings toward you? Do they love you or just tolerate you? Are they around you because they want to be or because they have to be? How might those feelings be changed if you were to stop using angry outbursts as a tool?

4. Do you find that your temper is getting hotter as you're getting older? Do you say and do things now in the heat of the moment that you wouldn't have considered a few years ago? If so, what do you think this means?

5. Make a list of ten things that really tick you off. Now go back through the list and identify each one as either a mountain or a molehill. (A mountain is a matter of grave importance where the health and well-being of people or the cause of Christ hangs in the balance. A molehill is a matter of lesser importance where, even if the worst were to happen, the damage done would be minimal and short-term.) What conclusion can you draw from this exercise?

CHAPTER SEVEN: STRONG MEN TEND TO REPEAT THE SAME MISTAKES

1. Do you have a besetting sin? What is it?

2. What has your besetting sin cost you? Can you name spe-

cific losses you've suffered because you keep making the same mistake?

3. Was there a time when your besetting sin bothered you more than it does now? Have you grown comfortable with it? Have you given up hope of ever defeating it? Have you begun to rationalize it? What rationalizations have you employed?

4. One of the keys to overcoming a besetting sin is to surrender completely to the Lord. What, specifically, do you need to change so that the Lord can assume more control of your life?

CHAPTER EIGHT: STRONG MEN TEND TO HAVE BIG EGOS

1. The Bible lists pride as a sin God hates, yet we know that God wants us to have healthy self-esteem. In your opinion, what are the primary differences between sinful pride and healthy self-esteem? Do you see any indications of either in your own life?

2. Think for a moment about your close friends. Do they tend to be people who are on or above your social level? Or do you have close friends who could never do anything to raise your status or advance your career? Is it important to you to be friends with influential people? Are you a name dropper?

3. Can you name something you used to take great pride in, but no longer do? What happened?

4. Is there something you're currently competing for? A job? A promotion? A woman? Explain why it's important to you to have it. How will your life change if you get it? How will you feel if you don't get it?

5. Have you ever had a "Nehemiah moment"? (Nehemiah had to choose between status and service.) If so, describe the choice

you were faced with and explain the decision you made. If you had it to do over again, would you choose differently?

CHAPTER NINE: STRONG MEN TEND TO TAKE FOOLISH RISKS

1. Can you name a risk you once took that you later realized was foolish? Can you explain why you took it? What was the result?
2. Can you name a risk you once took that you felt simply *had* to be taken? What made it seem so important? What was the result?
3. Can you name a tempting risk you once considered taking, but didn't? If so, why didn't you? How do you feel about it now? Do you feel you made a mistake or a good decision? If somehow you were to get another opportunity to do it, would you?
4. Think about David's elite soldiers who risked their lives to fetch him a drink of water from the well in Bethlehem. Have you ever taken a great risk for no other reason than love? How did it turn out?

CHAPTER TEN: STRONG MEN TEND TO STRUGGLE WITH INTIMACY

1. There are seven factors that inhibit intimacy in a strong man's marriage. They are: busyness, ambition, impatience, distraction, money, women, and fatigue. Which of these do you think your wife finds the most frustrating? Show the list to your wife and see if she concurs. Now sit down with her and talk about how you can make improvements in these areas.
2. When was the last time you did something romantic and totally unexpected for your wife? If it's been a while, can you

explain why? If you were to do something like that today, what would her reaction be? Right now, think of two or three romantic things you could do to surprise her.

3. Name your closest confidant, male or female, family member or friend. How long have you known this person? What is it about this individual that makes you feel so comfortable and willing to talk? Do you see those same attributes in yourself?

4. Name five things your wife loves to talk about. When was the last time *you* brought up one of those subjects? Pick the one you feel most comfortable with and think of a way to work it into a future conversation.

5. Make a list of things you and your wife share that are totally private . . . things that not another soul would know. You should be able to name at least five things. If you can't, you probably aren't respecting the privacy of your marriage the way you should. How can you do better in the future?

CHAPTER ELEVEN: STRONG MEN TEND TO TAKE TOO MUCH FOR GRANTED

1. Have you ever lost someone or something you thought you'd never lose? How did it happen? Do you believe you were somewhat responsible? What lessons did you learn?

2. Samson was betrayed by someone he assumed was on his side. Has that ever happened to you? What caused you to make that erroneous assumption? As a result of that experience, what changes have you made in the way you relate to people?

3. Think of some people your age or younger who have died from diseases or accidents. Picture their faces. Think of the days when they were still around. How does this make you

feel about your own mortality? How well have you been taking care of your health? How long has it been since you had a physical?

4. Have you ever been to a place or had an experience that made you more appreciative of your blessings? In what ways did that appreciation manifest itself? Has that appreciation since begun to fade again? Is there something you could do to regain it?

CHAPTER TWELVE: STRONG MEN TEND TO LOSE SIGHT OF THE BIG PICTURE

1. Samson was distracted from his life's purpose and never got around to doing the one thing God intended for him to do. How would you define your life's purpose? As far as you are concerned, what is the "big picture" that you always need to keep in view?

2. Think of a few things that bring you great pleasure. Have you given too much of your time, attention, or money to any of them? How would your wife or your closest friends answer that question?

3. A mission statement clearly states a company's ultimate purpose and is designed to prevent the company from drifting off course. Have you ever written a *personal* mission statement? If not, take some time and do it. Consider your passions, your talents, and God's will for your life.

4. Do you have a mentor or trusted spiritual advisor? If so, how has this person helped you in the past? If not, can you think of someone who might be able to assume that role? How good are you at taking advice? Would a mentor find you to be agreeable or argumentative?

5. Does your life need to have the fat trimmed out of it? Are you constantly doing things that are urgent, but not necessarily important? Do you find your time being eaten up by busy-work? If so, what specifically can you do to streamline your life so that you are able to focus on those things that are truly significant?

6. How often during a normal day do you think about God, heaven, or eternity? What are some things you could do to trigger more heavenly thoughts?

ABOUT THE AUTHOR

 MARK ATTEBERRY IS THE AWARD-winning author of eleven books and dozens of articles. You can follow him @mark_atteberry and read his blog at at alittlestrongereveryday.com. Since 1989, he has served as the preaching minister at Poinciana Christian Church in Kissimmee, Florida. When he isn't writing or preaching, Mark enjoys being a husband, father, and grandfather, and pursuing a variety of interests, including sports, playing the sax, and collecting jazz records.

ACKNOWLEDGMENTS

THE SAMSON SYNDROME WAS FIRST PUBLISHED BY Thomas Nelson in 2003. At the time, my acquisitions editor, Brian Hampton, said, "This book should have a long shelf life." Even in the face of such experience and optimism, I never dreamed we'd be repackaging it for another generation of readers eleven years later. I'm glad we are, though, because the lessons we can learn from Samson's life seem more relevant every day.

My publishing posse at Thomas Nelson has changed over the years, but is no less professional. In particular, Matt Baugher,

Adria Haley, and Andrea Lucado are especially gifted at publishing and promoting. Even more than that, I appreciate the fact that they are so nice. No author was ever treated better than I have been.

Eleven years ago, I thanked Linda Glasford, my agent at the time; the legendary Karen Kingsbury, who begged powerful people to read my work; Brian Hampton, who was the first editor to catch my vision; Pat Williams, of the Orlando Magic, who ballyhooed the original manuscript to everyone he knew; and Kyle Olund, who cleaned up my prose and made me seem like a better writer than I was. The collective spirit of all those wonderful people lives on in this new edition. I am no less thankful for their help than I ever was.

I must also thank my wife, Marilyn. Authors are quirky, as any author's spouse will tell you. She puts up with my blank stares, crazy hours, lightning bolt ideas, and rambling brainstorm sessions without complaint. I especially appreciate how she pretends it's all perfectly normal.

Finally, I'm grateful to my Heavenly Father. Everything I am, I owe to him. Please remember that all truth is His truth. Those of us who write books are merely scribes.